Also by Michael Leccese

Short Bike Rides™ in and around Washington, D.C.

Short Bike Rides™ in Colorado

by Michael Leccese

An East Woods Book

Old Saybrook, Connecticut

Photo Credits: P.4, Ed Kosmicki, *The Boulder Daily Camera;* pp. 10, 44, 98, 104, 112, Brian Anderson/*Estes Park Trail Gazette;* pp. 12, 28, 42, 48, Jamie Bloomquist/Outside Images; pp. 20, 66, Chatfield State Park/Colorado State Parks; p. 30, Mark Kiryluk; p. 34, *Fort Collins Coloradan;* p. 56, copyright © 1995 by Byron Hetzler/Winter Park; p. 58, copyright © 1990 by Carl Scofield/YMCA of the Rockies; p. 62, Mark Fox, *Summit Daily News;* p. 72, copyright © 1995 by Paul Gallaher; p. 80, Glenwood Springs Chamber of Commerce; pp. 92-93, Photosport; p. 100, Chris Marona/DACRA; p. 114, Rita Lucas Horvat/Colorado State Parks; p. 122, 124, Tom Stillo/Crested Butte Mountain Resort; p. 128, copyright © 1994 by John Young; p. 134, copyright © 1993 by James W. Jenson, Jr.; p. 142, Leadville Chamber of Commerce.

Short Bike Rides is a trademark of The Globe Pequot Press, Inc.

Library of Congress Cataloging-in-Publication Data

Leccese, Michael.
  Short bike rides in Colorado / by Michael Leccese.—1st ed.
      p.   cm.
  "An East Woods book."
  ISBN 1-56440-640-7
  1. Bicycle touring—Colorado—Guidebooks. 2. Colorado—Guidebooks. I. Title.
  GV1045.5.C6L43 1995
  796.6'4'09788—dc20   95-13956
                                                        CIP

♻ This book is printed on recycled paper.
Manufactured in the United States of America
First Edition/First Printing

In memory of
Victor A. Leccese (1924–1993),
who never rode a bike

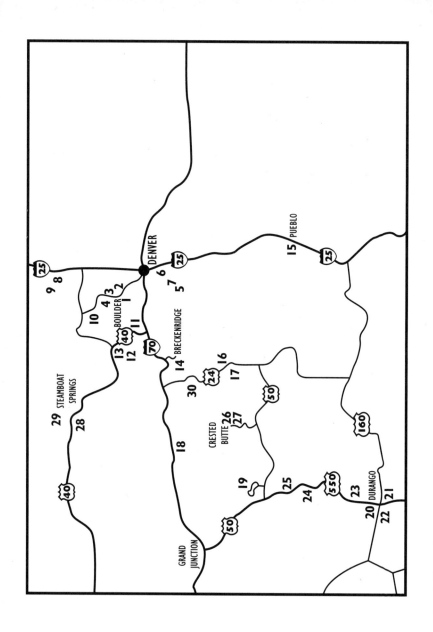

Contents

   * Good family ride
  ** Mountain bike recommended
*** Mountain bike required

Canyon Country

Durango Area

Ouray Area

Crested Butte Area

Steamboat Area

Leadville Area

   * Good family ride
  ** Mountain bike recommended
 *** Mountain bike required

Introduction

This book is designed for cyclists who *aren't* in training for the Olympics. Families out for day rides. Tourists making bicycling sorties into the Centennial State. Commuters seeking scenic routes. Mountain-bike owners ready to try off-road and single-track routes but not looking for a broken clavicle.

The rides included in this book are short (most under 30 miles), the grades undaunting (with exceptions), and opportunities to stop and dawdle plentiful. I road-tested about fifty routes in the summer of 1994. These thirty are the keepers. The mileage readings are as accurate as my Vetta bike computer. Many are family rides: Often I was hauling fifty pounds of bike trailer including Nora, our two-year-old.

In my younger days I viewed bicycling as an activity to be savored for its own sake. Now I'm careful to include destinations and diversions as part of any ride; I've tried to mention as many as possible in this book. While I enjoyed the physical challenge of pulling over Coal Bank Pass (elevation 10,600 feet) near Durango, for example, what I'll remember most about these trips is swimming with my daughter next to a prime trout-fishing hole in Lime Creek and floating in an inner tube at Strawberry Hot Springs within view of aspen glades.

I moved to Boulder in 1993 in part because Colorado is a cycling mecca. The state is a national magnet for all kinds of rides: rugged mountain biking among 14,000-foot peaks; road racing (the U.S. Cycling Federation is headquartered in Colorado Springs); cross-state touring; and casual rides on 800 miles of paved urban trails. Trips can range from easy (the 16-mile paved path out of the spa town of Glenwood Springs) to murderous (the 470-mile off-road Colorado Trail, which crosses the Continental Divide a dozen times). Some twenty ski towns, from Aspen to Winter Park, now open their Nordic trails for summer mountain biking (located just ninety minutes by car west of Denver, Winter Park has 600 miles of such trails). The U.S. Forest Service maintains 6,000 miles of off-road trails on public lands. With a population of about 90,000, the college/high-tech town of Boulder boasts more registered bikes than cars. In southwestern Colorado, Durango hosts world-class mountain biking. Areas like Jefferson

County and Crested Butte base chunks of their tourist economies on catering to bikers.

And here's a surprise: The climate is conducive to cycling. On the high prairie in the shadow of the Rockies, cycling is possible and enjoyable on all but very snowy days. Hence, Boulder, Fort Collins, and Denver have some of the United States' highest rates of bicycle commuting. Mountain areas are more limited to an April-to-November season, but certain sun-washed canyons and valleys make year round rides possible up to 9,000 feet.

Colorado also hosts dozens of velo-events, including three cross-mountain rides that attract thousands of participants in May and June. The state supports a bicycling coordinator and fifteen cycling organizations (see Appendix). Destinations for cyclists include historic mining towns, hot springs, and Colorado Rockies baseball games. Some skiers even bike to the slopes.

A number of rides in this book can be accomplished astride anything with wheels: road bike, mountain bike, or in-line skates. I've included several rides just for mountain bikers, however. These include Jeep roads, dirt roads, and single-track unpaved paths. Most are for novices. I've also suggested good bets for in-line skating or for bringing the family.

It is my hope that this book will help you to enjoy our state without burning fossil fuels. As a booming state in a sprawling region, Colorado experiences some of the automobile-related woes that I was trying to escape on the East Coast: noise, air pollution, and pavement everywhere. It doesn't have to be like that—in Boulder, our car is practically mothballed. We bike to market, daycare, work, hiking trailheads, and so on. You too might discover that your bicycle is a healthful, safe, pleasurable alternative to driving.

Before You Bike: Be Prepared

Cycling in Colorado presents some challenges.
- **Altitude:** Even the fittest flatlanders may wheeze their first time over a 10,000-foot pass. Give yourself a few days to acclimate before exercising at the same intensity that you're accustomed to at

lower elevations. Carry two full water bottles, and drink fluids whenever you can. (One rule of thumb: If you never feel the urge to urinate during a ride, you're not taking in enough liquid.)

- **Quick-Change Weather**: You can be hit by snow, hail, or gelid rain at almost any time in the mountains. Even in Boulder it can snow in September or May. Summer thunderstorms roll in at laser speed. Things to carry on most rides include warm winter leggings, waterproof jacket, gloves with fingers, camping matches or a cigarette lighter, and perhaps a lightweight Mylar blanket to wrap around yourself if your body temperature seems to be dropping (signs of hypothermia: wooziness, chattering teeth, uncontrollable shivering). Also carry a phone card. Don't be afraid to hitchhike if you're in trouble: Colorado's pickup-driving masses are generally happy to ferry cyclists out of a storm.

- **Old Man Sol**: The sun shines 300 days a year here—not good news if you worry about skin melanoma. Skip right past prissy sunscreens and go right to the blocks rated twenty-five SPF or above. In June and July try to schedule rides before 10:00 A.M. and after 3:00 P.M. Get decent, UV-protection sunglasses. Pick rides that offer shade.

- **The Roads**: Put fifty-six peaks over 14,000 feet in a single state and what do you have? Very few places to build roads. Route planning is essential unless you like sharing a narrow canyon with a phalanx of RVs en route to an Airstream convention. (Note: Bicycles are not allowed on certain roads.)

  There are alternatives to competing with traffic. One allure of mountain biking is that it eliminates *all* cars. The state also boasts many lightly traveled dirt roads; mountain bikes are handy here, but often not essential. Finally, the urban bikeway has become a Colorado standard. Beautifully laid out, smooth concrete pathways grace Boulder, Denver, Fort Collins, Breckenridge, Frisco, Pueblo, Vail, and Steamboat Springs. This book introduces many of these rides.

- **Safety**: Wear a helmet at all times. Buy brightly colored cycling togs (you might look good in hot pink) visible to motorists from hundreds of yards away. Carry a U-lock. Mount lights on your bike, front and rear. Bring maps and raingear. Ride with a buddy. Practice safe cycling techniques: Pump brakes (don't lock them) going down mountains; brake with your rear brakes (right-hand lever) first; obey traffic laws; on roads, learn to ride in an arrow-straight line; on single-track mountain trails, keep within your abilities and walk your bike if necessary.

Acknowledgments

Thanks to those who suggested routes and helped me map them out, including Russel Bollig, Woody Eaton, Michael Maisonpierre, Angela McCormick, and Dan Platt. Special thanks to my wife, Kathleen Mc-Cormick, and Nora, our daughter, for their company, patience, and support.

The following people also helped by providing information or photographs: Brian Anderson, *Estes Park Trail Gazette;* Craig Bergman, Lory State Park; Jamie Bloomquist, Outside Images; Leslie Bohm, Catalyst Communications; Ira Curry, Chaffee County Visitors Bureau; Z. James Czupor, the InterPro Group; Dean Dennis, Pueblo Chamber of Commerce; Deborah Duke, Colorado State Parks; Julien Foreman, Glenwood Springs Chamber Resort Association; Mark Fox, *Summit Daily News;* Byron Hetzler, Winter Park Resort; Scott Hobson, Summit County Planning; Nancy Kramer, Steamboat Arts Council; Patti McCarthy, Durango Area Chamber Resort Association; Stuart McDonald, Colorado State Parks; Gay Page, *Bicycle Colorado;* Andrea Robbins, Go Boulder; Douglass Shaw; Bill Wenk, Wenk Associates, Denver; Chris Wilson, Steamboat Springs Parks Department; Laura Wilson, Crested Butte Mountain Resort; Kent Young, Boulder Off-Road Alliance; Paul Zanger, Black Canyon National Monument.

Special thanks to my editor, Laura Strom, at Globe Pequot, for smoothly shepherding yet another project.

Boulder's Bikeways

Distance:	16 miles (with options, 20 or 22 miles)
Approximate pedaling time:	90 minutes
Terrain:	Flat
Surface:	Top-notch paved bikeways, 2-lane road
Things to see:	Downtown Boulder, town open space, University Hill
Facilities:	All downtown
Options:	Rides to Marshall Mesa (single-track) and Eldorado State Park

Having lived in Boulder for a while now, I have concluded that this college town's reputation as bicycling nirvana is well deserved. Perfect, no, but Boulder is one of the few places in the United States where the bicycle is taken seriously as transportation. There are 60 miles of off-road trails and on-road lanes, and people ride them in all seasons. It's not uncommon to attend any kind of public event—a planning hearing or a party—and find a sizable number of folks show up in Lycra tights and helmets. About 7 percent of Boulderites commute to work on bikes, a figure that is at least seven times the national average and not bad for a place where it snows two dozen times a year. Sometimes it's hard to find a bicycle parking space downtown.

This tour takes you through the core of Boulder's custom-made bikeways: smooth and sinuous cement paths that emanate from the spine of Boulder Creek. This sojourn across prairie and suburb is a wonderful midday escape, with excellent views of the Front Range and Continental Divide. It also serves practical purposes. You can take the trail to discount hypermarkets, movie theaters, public pools,

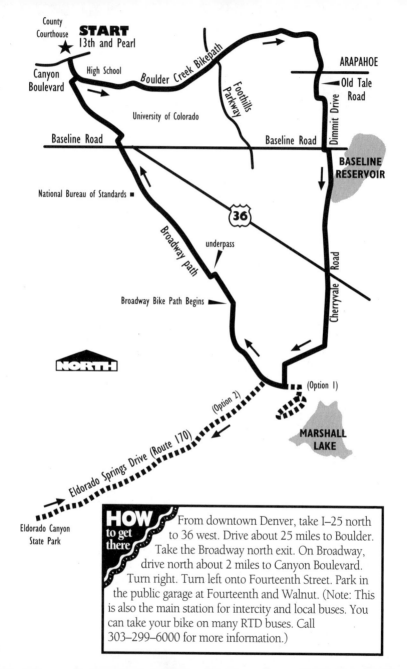

County Courthouse

START
13th and Pearl

Canyon Boulevard

High School

Boulder Creek Bikepath

ARAPAHOE

Old Tale Road

Foothills Parkway

Dimmit Drive

University of Colorado

Baseline Road

Baseline Road

BASELINE RESERVOIR

National Bureau of Standards ■

36

Broadway path

underpass

Broadway Bike Path Begins ▶

Cherryvale Road

NORTH

(Option 1)

(Option 2)

MARSHALL LAKE

Eldorado Springs Drive (Route 170)

Eldorado Canyon State Park

HOW to get there   From downtown Denver, take I–25 north to 36 west. Drive about 25 miles to Boulder. Take the Broadway north exit. On Broadway, drive north about 2 miles to Canyon Boulevard. Turn right. Turn left onto Fourteenth Street. Park in the public garage at Fourteenth and Walnut. (Note: This is also the main station for intercity and local buses. You can take your bike on many RTD buses. Call 303–299–6000 for more information.)

DIREC-TIONS at a glance

0.0 Start at Thirteenth and Pearl in downtown Boulder. Head south on the separate bike lane.

0.2 After crossing Canyon Boulevard, take right onto bike path.

0.2 Turn left at T intersection of bike paths.

0.3 Go straight at bike-path intersection.

2.6 After underpass for Foothills Parkway, turn left at bike-path intersection to cross footbridge.

3.1 Turn right at T intersection.

4.0 Bear left at path intersection.

4.1 Bear left at path intersection.

5.2 After crossing under Arapahoe Road near Subaru dealership, pathway ends at Old Tale Road.

5.2 Turn left onto Old Tale Road.

5.4 Old Tale dead-ends. Go straight to pick up Centennial hiker/biker trail.

5.8 Trail ends. Go straight on Dimmit Drive.

6.0 Turn right onto Cherryvale Road.

10.1 Turn right onto Marshall Road.

Option 1: From Cherryvale Road, go past Marshall Road and take next left onto Marshall Drive to the Marshall Open Space (single-track), a 4-mile round-trip.

Option 2: From Marshall Road, turn left at Route 170 in Marshall for a 6-mile round-trip to Eldorado Canyon State Park.

11.6 Marshall Road ends at Broadway bikeway. Go straight.

13.5 Left to underpass beneath Broadway.

14.6 After crossing Baseline Road at light, turn right to underpass beneath Broadway.

15.7 Near Boulder Creek, turn left at T intersection of bike path.

15.8 At four-way bike intersection, turn left (sign reads TO NORTH 13TH STREET).

15.8 Turn left onto Thirteenth Street.

16.0 Return to start at Thirteenth and Pearl.

a major university, playgrounds, a recycling center, and used-car dealerships—and people do.

Start downtown at Thirteenth and Pearl streets. Head north on the new downtown bikeway, a dedicated lane separated from traffic by huge concrete planters. The city's decision to build the bikeway was gutsy, since it required elimination of thirty-three parking spaces for cars. (Downtown merchants are still howling.) After a couple of city blocks, turn right near Boulder Creek to gain access to the trail. This site, at Thirteenth and Canyon, hosts the state's largest farmers' market, from April through October.

At a trail intersection turn left to head east along Boulder Creek. This is a busy section with a posted speed limit: 10 mph. The creekway is heavily wooded and separate from traffic for the next 60 blocks. At Twenty-sixth Street you can stop and view the creek through a subterranean plate-glass window. There's a healthy trout habitat here, and catch-and-release fishing is encouraged. A spot near the Twenty-eighth Street underpass is popular for wading and swimming. If you want to do laps or play tennis, try Scott Carpenter Park, near the Thirtieth Street interchange.

The Great Plains unfold east of Thirtieth, and you'll see many prairie-dog towns along the path. Here the views of glaciers open up as the speed limit increases to 25 mph. Boulder is the place in the United States where prairie and glaciers are closest to each other: about 20 miles. You can switch habitats and environs here the way most people change their shoes. A trail section threads through lakes that become a busy "Manhattan" for geese in winter. Then it swings north for sweeping views of the Continental Divide.

When the trail ends after Fifty-fifth Street, you don't need to retrace your steps to town. Follow the directions to Cherryvale Road for a two-lane romp through ranch- and farmland, then return to town via Marshall, a former mining burg that seems not to have changed much since the last canary died. There's an optional single-track spin around the Marshall Mesa open space here (see map and directions), or a left down Route 170 will take you to Eldorado Canyon State Park, a major gorge and climbing mecca just south of town. The park was once a resort where, in 1915, Dwight and Mamie

5

Eisenhower spent their honeymoon. A springs-fed public pool, open in summer, is a remnant of that era.

If you don't take any detours, proceed north on the Broadway path through suburban Boulder and up to University Hill. If you explore the campus, lock your bike on "the Hill" near Thirteenth Street. Most University of Colorado paths are off limits to bikes. Considered one of the prettiest state campuses in the United States, CU is built almost entirely from Lyons sandstone in an Italianate style. An exception is the quadrangle, lined by red-brick, turreted buildings from the Victorian era.

Back on the trail, take care. The Broadway trail is well delineated (and it features a gorgeous underpass designed by Oz Architects), but caffeine-fired students take little heed of its rules. Scream downhill past a small arboretum. The path snakes down to the playing fields of Boulder High and returns you to downtown.

The Poorman Connection:
From Downtown to the Mountains

Distance:	11 miles round-trip
Approximate pedaling time:	1 hour
Terrain:	Long, steady climb followed by a swift descent
Surface:	Paved and gravel bike paths, paved 2-lane road, dirt road, city streets
Things to see:	Boulder Creek bikeway, Boulder Canyon, mountain views, Sunshine Canyon, historic Mapleton Hill neighborhood, downtown Boulder
Facilities:	Restrooms, restaurants, etc., in town

This is my favorite midweek escape from my office cubicle in downtown Boulder: a ride that encompasses everything from downtown bars to mountaintop bird sanctuaries in exactly one hour.

Start at the intersection of Thirteenth Street and the Pearl Street Mall, a 4-block section closed to auto traffic. This elaborately landscaped promenade is the city's commercial, governmental, and entertainment heart. Heading north on Thirteenth Street (the mountains are visible on your left), you pass the ziggurat of the Boulder County Courthouse, an Art Deco concoction built in 1934 from cream-colored stone salvaged from an abandoned railroad bridge. In 2 blocks turn left onto Pine Street. The fine red-brick building is the historic Hotel Boulderado, just restored in recent years.

Now you're heading west through Mapleton Hill, home to historic residences. With its tall trees and grand, multigabled houses, the street resembles something out of Brookline, Massachusetts. At Fourth Street, turn right and take the first left onto Mapleton. The

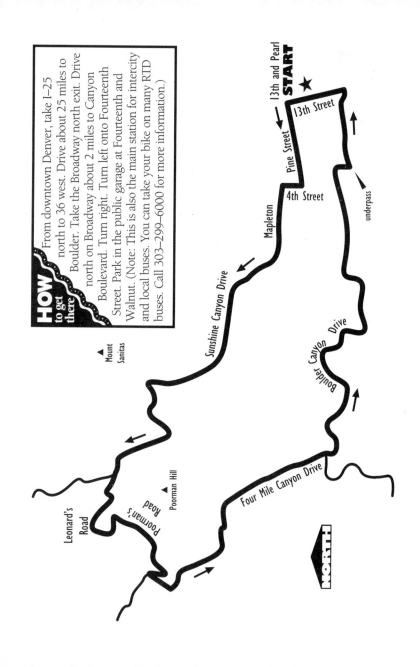

HOW to get there

From downtown Denver, take I-25 north to 36 west. Drive about 25 miles to Boulder. Take the Broadway north exit. Drive north on Broadway about 2 miles to Canyon Boulevard. Turn right. Turn left onto Fourteenth Street. Park in the public garage at Fourteenth and Walnut. (Note: This is also the main station for intercity and local buses. You can take your bike on many RTD buses. Call 303-299-6000 for more information.)

Mount Sanitas

Sunshine Canyon Drive

Mapleton

Pine Street

13th and Pearl
START

13th Street

4th Street

underpass

Boulder Canyon Drive

Leonard's Road

Poorman's Road

Poorman Hill

Four Mile Canyon Drive

NORTH

DIREC-TIONS at a glance

0.0 Start in downtown Boulder at Thirteenth and Pearl. Head north on Thirteenth Street.

0.2 Turn left onto Pine Street.

0.7 Turn right onto Fourth Street.

0.8 Turn left onto Mapleton (becomes Sunshine Canyon Drive).

3.5 Turn left onto Poorman's Road.

5.5 Turn left onto Four Mile Canyon Drive.

7.5 Cross Boulder Canyon Drive, turn left onto bike path.

10.8 Turn left onto Thirteenth Street (north).

11.0 Arrive at Thirteenth and Pearl.

two-lane road begins to rise and the townhouses fade away as you climb into Sunshine Canyon, a land of sere grasses and ponderosa pine. You pass the Dakota Ridge, a hogback rock formation demarcating the line between prairie and foothills. The trailhead to Mount Sanitas (no bikes allowed) is on your right.

Climb a few switchbacks and busy Boulder becomes just a memory. The view is of surprisingly soft mountains layered with ponderosa pine. It's not uninhabited, but the houses tend toward the large and well spaced, and traffic is pretty light. Soon the backlighted glaciers of the Continental Divide come into view, practically instant gratification after only twenty minutes of climbing. The canyon is well named: Its ample sunshine makes this section a year-round ride.

As you pass dirt roads adjoining Sunshine Canyon Drive, keep track of signs on your left. At mile 3.5, just when the route threatens to go vertical, turn left onto Poorman's Road. For 2 miles Poorman's twists dramatically down. Leonard's Road, on your right, envelops a small bird sanctuary, where I've seen bluebirds and hawks. Poorman's comes to a T. Turn left on this paved road to head down Four Mile Canyon, bordered by a creek and high rock walls.

In another 2 miles, Four Mile Canyon ends in a T at Boulder Canyon Drive. Carefully cross this busy road to adjoin the Boulder

Canyon Trail, an unpaved hiker/biker route coursing down Boulder Creek. The canyon is the hip place to bike, walk, rock climb, and birdwatch, so expect crowds in good weather and on weekends. There are also fishing holes and remains of earlier mining, railroad, and water-supply structures along the way. (Note: This 2-mile section is unplowed in winter.)

From the edge of town, a paved path brings you back into Boulder amid the shade of cottonwood trees. On your left, the creek may be full of kayakers running a specially designed course, inner-tubers, and swimmers. The trail runs below grade at cross streets, so you never deal with auto traffic. You pass a sculpture garden, xeriscape (low-water) demonstration garden, fish ponds, a playground, and the city's snazzy new library. Near an outdoor amphitheater, turn left at a four-way bicycle intersection where a sign marks 13TH STREET NORTH. In 3 blocks you're back downtown. Lock up and go have a latte.

When I last did this ride, it was a humid day with hazy ridges and no one around. The aspens were showing the first signs of fall after a long, dry summer. Purple wildflowers bloomed along the roadside. I saw hummingbirds, bluebirds, and a herd of mule deer, including bucks with full, fuzzy racks. (In town the Lycra lizards were elbowing for space on the bike path.) It's not a good ride for kids, adults hauling trailers, or in-line skates.

Bustop and Back

Distance:	27 miles
Approximate pedaling time:	2 hours
Terrain:	Pretty flat
Surface:	2-lane roads with and without shoulders
Things to see:	Nobody rides this for the scenery
Facilities:	All in central Boulder

The Bustop Ride represents the "dark side to Boulder's bicycling force," reported *Sports Illustrated* in 1993. Not only is it named for the county's only topless bar (waggishly dubbed the Boulder Center for the Terpsichorean Arts), but for years it attracted as many as a hundred racers-in-training all dressed like some combination of a bumblebee and Robocop. This swarm hogged a major north–south route by riding in slipstream packs, twice a week, at 5:00 P.M., like clockwork.

Beet-faced drivers howled, and police finally cracked down with a Bastille Day 1987 sting operation employing airplanes, video cameras, and eight patrol cars to nab offenders. Then the county passed a ride-single-file law, which extends to many county roads. Racers responded in the winter of 1994 by setting up their own 1.1-mile course near the Stazio Fields in east Boulder.

That's the modern-day outlaw lore behind this quick escape and perfect tune-up for adult cyclists of all levels. Start at Thirteenth and Pearl streets on the downtown mall. Head north for a few miles through unpretentious (albeit expensive) neighborhoods. A paved path detours along the edge of Long's Iris Farms, a cheerful anachronism amid booming Boulder. Pick up Broadway north to traverse

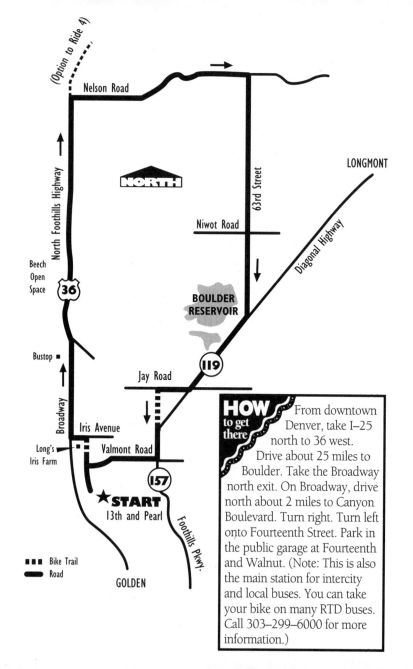

(Option to Ride 4)

Nelson Road

NORTH

LONGMONT

North Foothills Highway

63rd Street

Niwot Road

Diagonal Highway

Beech
Open
Space

36

**BOULDER
RESERVOIR**

Bustop ■

119

Jay Road

Broadway

Iris Avenue

Long's
Iris Farm

Valmont Road

157

★**START**
13th and Pearl

Foothills Pkwy.

■■■ Bike Trail
▬▬ Road

GOLDEN

HOW
to get
there
From downtown
Denver, take I–25
north to 36 west.
Drive about 25 miles to
Boulder. Take the Broadway
north exit. On Broadway, drive
north about 2 miles to Canyon
Boulevard. Turn right. Turn left
onto Fourteenth Street. Park in
the public garage at Fourteenth
and Walnut. (Note: This is also
the main station for intercity
and local buses. You can take
your bike on many RTD buses.
Call 303–299–6000 for more
information.)

DIREC-TIONS at a glance

0.0	Start at Thirteenth and Pearl in downtown Boulder. Head north on Thirteenth Street.
1.0	Thirteenth Street ends. Pick up bikeway past Boulder Rec Center and Long's Iris Farm.
1.2	Turn left onto Iris Avenue.
1.3	Turn right onto Broadway.
4.0	Turn left onto Route 36 (North Foothills Highway).
9.5	Turn right onto Nelson Road.
13.8	Turn right onto Sixty-third Street.
19.3	Turn right onto Diagonal Highway (Route 119).
22.0	Turn right onto Jay Road.
22.5	Turn left onto Forty-seventh Street (becomes trail along Foothills Parkway, Route 157).
24.0	Turn right onto Valmont Road (becomes Balsam Avenue at Twenty-sixth Street).
26.0	Turn left onto Thirteenth Street at four-way stop.
27.0	Return to start at Thirteenth and Pearl.

Option

To connect with the Carter Lake Escape (ride 4), continue north up Route 36 (North Foothills Highway) 3.5 miles to Hygiene Road. Turn right and proceed 4 miles to Hygiene Town Center.

suburban neighborhoods and then a light-industrial area, with trailer parks, second hand shops, an armory, and The Bustop nightclub. After that dive through the fringes, turn left onto U.S. 36. The view unfolds endlessly into tawny foothills.

What happened to the slurb? For nearly eighty-five years, Boulder has been buying and locking up open space like this, spurred on by a 1910 report by landscape architect Frederick Law Olmsted, Jr. Today Boulder's 30,000 acres of open space attract as many visitors as some national parks: 1.5 million a year. With success comes new problems;

now the city grapples with issues of overuse. Mountain bikes have already been banned from most open space west of Broadway.

Keep your eyes on the road for this busy stretch of Route 36 north (a.k.a. the North Foothills Highway), with the Dakota Hogback rock formation and the Beech Open Space on your left. A wide shoulder makes this a pretty safe shot. The full Bustop ride would take you into Hygiene (an option achieved by combining this ride with ride 4).

After passing clusters of fancy-schmancy houses, turn right at Nelson Road to lose traffic and start gliding east onto the prairie. I did this on a July evening, watching hawks silhouetted against a full moon rising. The knoll on the right is Table Mountain, used by the federal government for antennae fields. Nelson rolls (the prairie isn't flat because it's former ocean bottom lined with marine fossils) through some pastureland until you hit Sixty-third Street, a southern route back toward town. The route is pocked with reservoirs small and large that make excellent wildlife habitat. You're sure to see prairie dogs and might spot white pelicans skimming Boulder Reservoir.

The Boulder-Longmont Diagonal leads into town on a very wide shoulder. A combination of on-road lanes and off-road trails returns you to central Boulder.

Carter Lake Escape

Distance:	30.6 miles
Approximate pedaling time:	2–3 hours
Terrain:	Rolling prairie
Surface:	2-lane blacktop
Things to see:	Quiet farmland against a mountain backdrop
Facilities:	Country store in Hygiene

This is a favorite getaway road-bike ride for the increasingly urban denizens of Boulder. You'll pass through quiet farm- and ranchland that seems more like a remnant of quieter, more rural times as the Front Range attracts growing numbers of people (like me) seeking the good life closer to nature.

This tour is rideable from Boulder (see ride 3) if you can put up with a narrow section of Route 36. It's more enjoyable begun in tiny Hygiene, a farming community about a dozen miles north of Boulder. Early settlers were Germans who organized the Church of the Brethren, or Dunkard Church, named for the practice of baptizing new members in the St. Vrain River. A former sanitarium, the Hygiene Home, gave the town its name in the 1880s. Don't go looking for the home; it failed as a business venture and was razed in 1926.

Park at Clark's, a country store on Seventy-fifth Street. Head north to busy, four-lane Route 66, where a wide shoulder offers some security. Heading east on 66, turn left onto Eighty-seventh Street, heading north. Wind along farm roads edged by llama ranches, sagebrush, and fields of mown hay. You'll see cottonwoods that would require three men to embrace and ponds frequented by white pelicans in summer. Just west is Rabbit Mountain, a county-owned open space where prairie-dog towns attract plenty of raptors looking for a meal.

17

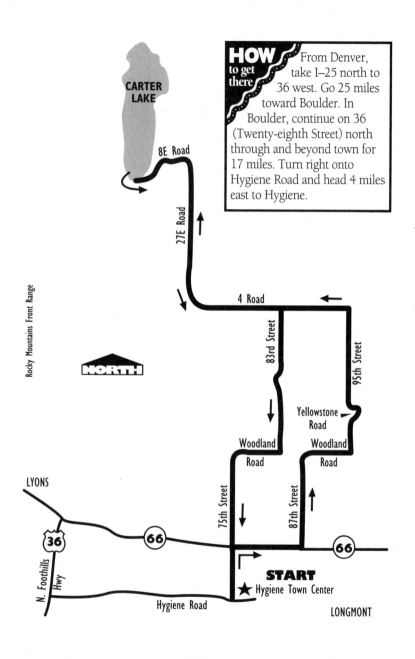

CARTER LAKE

HOW to get there — From Denver, take I–25 north to 36 west. Go 25 miles toward Boulder. In Boulder, continue on 36 (Twenty-eighth Street) north through and beyond town for 17 miles. Turn right onto Hygiene Road and head 4 miles east to Hygiene.

8E Road

27E Road

4 Road

83rd Street

95th Street

Rocky Mountains Front Range

NORTH

Yellowstone Road

Woodland Road

Woodland Road

75th Street

87th Street

LYONS

36
N. Foothills Hwy

66

66

START
★ Hygiene Town Center

Hygiene Road

LONGMONT

DIREC-TIONS at a glance

0.0 Start in Hygiene at Clark's country store on Seventy-fifth Street.

1.0 Turn right onto Route 66 (Ute Road).

2.5 Turn left onto Eighty-seventh Street.

4.5 Turn right onto Woodland Road.

5.5 Turn left onto Ninety-fifth Street.

6.5 Turn left onto Yellowstone Road.

6.6 Turn right on Ninety-fifth Street.

8.6 Turn left onto Country Road 4.

13.6 Bear right at 27E Road.

16.6 Turn left onto 8E Road.

17.6 Arrive at Carter Lake Reservoir. Turn around and retrace to Country Road 4.

23.6 Turn right onto Blue Mountain Road (becomes Eighty-third Street).

26.6 Turn right onto Woodland Road.

27.6 Turn left onto Seventy-fifth Street.

29.6 Cross Route 66 to continue straight on Seventy-fifth Street.

30.6 Return to start.

Magpies and western meadowlarks criss-cross the road as you head into Larimer County. These roads stay pretty clear for winter rides, when hawks and eagles perch on telephone poles.

The last couple of miles up to Carter Lake present the only real climb (about 400 feet) on a dirt/gravel road. The ride back toward Hygiene offers a tour of tidy, German-inspired barns and farmhouses with views of Longs Peak, a 14er whose 2,000-foot granite visage gleams like sapphire. Crossing Route 66 again, turn right, and detour down the road a mile if you want to see Lyons. This sturdy quarrying-and-tourism town, cleaved by the St. Vrain River, hosts summer bluegrass and folk festivals. The red-rock walls of St. Vrain Canyon provide perfect acoustics.

I did the ride on a balmy summer night and enjoyed every crank. However, I was glad I didn't have my daughter along, due to narrow or nonexistent shoulders on some of these country lanes.

Waterton Wayfarer

Distance:	6.2 miles each way
Approximate pedaling time:	2 hours
Terrain:	Slight elevation gain into river canyon
Surface:	A dirt road smooth enough for road bikes
Things to see:	Quiet canyon walls, South Platte River, bighorn sheep
Facilities:	Restrooms at both ends of trail

Waterton Canyon provides access to one of the state's toughest rides: the 470-mile Colorado Trail, which crosses the Continental Divide numerous times en route to Durango.

This is a relatively easy 6.2-mile ramble down a wide, auto-free dirt road, however, which offers as much scenic bang for your caloric buck as any ride in this book. Rising only about 100 feet a mile, this former railroad bed hastens away from Denver's urbanized fringe into a wildlife-rich canyon where you can't see, hear, or sense the city.

Start in a parking lot next to the Kassler Treatment Plant, a complex of square concrete ponds and antique clapboard buildings that is a landmark among waterworks. It was the first sand-based water-filtration plant built west of the Mississippi. Walk your bike through a turnstile and begin riding along a rocky, natural-looking (but actually much dammed and diverted) section of the South Platte River.

The high prairie quickly recedes as craggy canyon walls rise steeply. The rock colors are sere, dusty-red sandstone, ashen. Yet there's fairly lush riparian and subalpine vegetation, including ponderosa pine, mountain juniper, and gambel or scrub oak (a fall favorite in screaming red). When I visited in early fall, trees were still

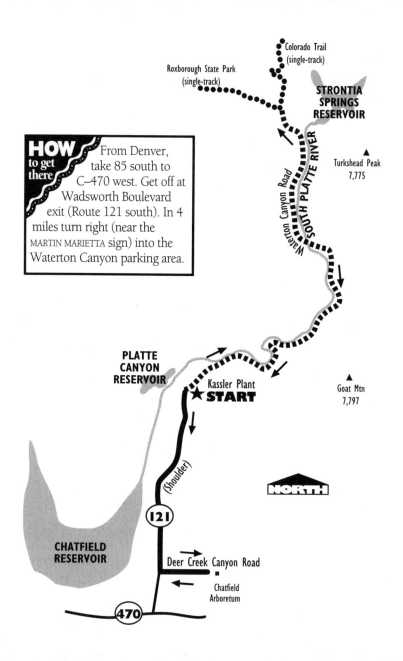

Colorado Trail
(single-track)

Roxborough State Park
(single-track)

**STRONTIA
SPRINGS
RESERVOIR**

HOW *to get there* From Denver, take 85 south to C–470 west. Get off at Wadsworth Boulevard exit (Route 121 south). In 4 miles turn right (near the MARTIN MARIETTA sign) into the Waterton Canyon parking area.

Turkshead Peak
7,775

Waterton Canyon Road

SOUTH PLATTE RIVER

**PLATTE
CANYON
RESERVOIR**

Kassler Plant
START

Goat Mtn
7,797

(Shoulder)

NORTH

121

**CHATFIELD
RESERVOIR**

Deer Creek Canyon Road

Chatfield
Arboretum

470

DIREC-TIONS at a glance

0.0 Start at parking lot for Kassler Treatment Plant. Walk bike through turnstile.

6.2 Trail ends near Strontia Springs Dam. Retrace steps to start.

Option

To reach Chatfield Arboretum, turn left out of parking lot onto Route 121 (wide shoulder). In 4 miles turn left at sign for ARBORETUM.

green. The rabbitbrush varied from vibrant yellow to dusty. These desert shrubs were virtually covered with black-and-gold butterfly moths. There were bikers of all ages out. Many had fishing gear strapped to their frames. Everyone rode a mountain bike.

The river alternately tumbles and glazes over. You pass a caretaker's house, several side gulches, and pulley bridges set up so that water engineers can reach their equipment. The tallest peak to the right is Turkshead, elevation 7,775 feet. Pike National Forest is on the left. At the trailtop look down a side canyon at Strontia Springs Dam, 243 feet of concrete poured in 1983. Sadly, the dam placed Stevens Gulch, another nice section of canyon, in a watery grave. Strontia Springs formerly hosted a hot-springs resort that could be reached by the Denver, South Park, and Pacific Railroads.

We met people who had just seen bighorn sheep. A rare low-elevation herd of about thirty lives and breeds within the canyon, as do a few dozen bird species, elk, mule deer, mountain lion, and rattlesnake. We didn't meet any 300-pound *Ovis canadensis*, but we did have a nice chat with a couple who live nearby. They said that the canyon road is rideable every month of the year. Trail gates are open from 4:00 A.M.to 9:00 P.M.year-round.

Near Strontia Springs Dam an option is to try a short, easy, single-track mountain-bike loop that offers a small sample of Colorado Trail. Another option: Back at the parking lot, head down the broad shoulder of Route 121 for 4 miles to visit the Chatfield Arboretum of the Denver Botanic Gardens. This 700-acre complex includes a restored one-room schoolhouse and preserved remains of two early Colorado farms, along with wetlands, rock gardens, giant cottonwoods, and a "survival garden" showing plants used by Indians and early settlers. It's a great place to learn about the state and your own garden at the same time.

Downtown Express

Distance:	29 miles round-trip
Approximate pedaling time:	3 hours
Terrain:	Flat
Surface:	Paved bike path
Things to see:	Downtown Denver, Cherry Creek, Four-Mile House historic farm, Cherry Creek State Park
Facilities:	Restrooms at Four-Mile House, all facilities at state park

"Denver's getting better" is the mantra you'll hear among boosterish Front Rangers. This ride demonstrates that Denver's cow-town reputation is giving way to big-city panache. One indication: In 1989 residents approved a bond issue that provides $242 million for park improvements, including greenway and bike paths.

The spiffy Cherry Creek Bikeway is already one of the city's best routes. Start the ride at Creekfront Park, near the spot where Cherry Creek and the Platte River meet. This new park is a people place enlivened by steps down to the river, a wading pool planted with papyrus, and colorful, petroglyph-inspired sculptures by artist Bill Gian. The overall design is by landscape architect William Wenk. You're not far from Denver's revitalized (and bikeable) Lower Downtown, a former warehouse district that's home to dozens of art galleries, Elitch's amusement park, and Coors Field baseball stadium.

The ride courses away from downtown on a smooth trail running parallel to Speer Boulevard, named for a master-building mayor. At first the view ain't much: Cherry Creek is contained in a channel below grade from the street. Mostly you're looking at concrete retain-

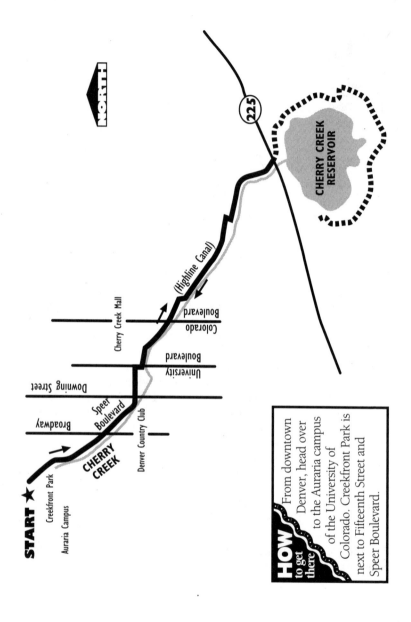

DIREC-TIONS at a glance		
	0.0	Start at Creekfront Park, near Fifteenth Street and the Auraria Campus in downtown Denver.
	0.3	Bicycle and pedestrian paths merge.
	2.7	Trail becomes a sidewalk parallel to First Avenue (Denver Country Club is on your right).
	3.4	Cross University Boulevard at light (Cherry Creek Mall at left).
9.0		Bear right at sign for Highline Canal.
9.5		Turn left to stay on Highline Canal Trail.
14.5		Arrive at Cherry Creek State Park. Retrace steps to start the following option.

Option

Semi-loop ride of several miles around reservoir on park road.

---

ing walls. Dive-bombing swallows and other cyclists serve to amuse until you pass Denver Country Club, when the creek opens up into a cottonwood-lined stream. To the left is Cherry Creek Mall, the state's number-one tourist attraction. (Does that thought depress you? Head a few blocks over to the vast Tattered Cover Bookstore, a bibliophile's Eden, for intellectual recharge.)

Farther along, Four-Mile Historic Park offers a look at nineteenth-century rural life. The fourteen-acre complex includes Denver's oldest house, bee houses, barns with draft horses, apple orchards, and a garden with antique roses.

Around mile 9, bear right at a fork toward the Highline Canal Trail. That's right, *derecha, droit.* I mistakenly bore left and got lost in industrial parks for 15 miles. It didn't help when I stopped on a lawn to regain my bearings. A pop-up sprinkler reared, spraying me and my map, which disintegrated.

The Highline (which runs all the way to Waterton Canyon; see the Waterton Wayfarer ride, chapter 5) speeds you toward Cherry

Creek State Park: 4,700 acres of dense recreation, including birding, camping, and 880 acres of water surface. After passing some condos and a golf course, gingerly cross Highway 225 at a light and proceed about a mile toward the park entrance on the right. If you turn right too soon, you'll wind up on a narrow dead-end road high atop an earthen dam. A better option is to continue half a mile to the park proper ($3.00 admission fee in 1995) and take the loop around Cherry Creek Reservoir. You can accomplish this either on 8 miles of off-road paths or on the main park road, a favorite training ride for Denverites.

Cherry Creek, Colorado's first state park (founded in 1960), includes cottonwood groves, prairie-dog towns, wetlands, and more than thirty different recreation activities. The reservoir site was originally part of the Smoky Hill Trail, which carried stagecoaches and claim-seekers to the gold fields between 1859 and 1865.

Expect crowds on this ride. For good reason, the path is popular among racers, in-line skaters, and family riders alike.

A Circle Around Chatfield Reservoir

Distance:	12-mile loop
Approximate pedaling time:	90 minutes
Terrain:	Rolling prairie
Surface:	Cement bike path
Things to see:	South Platte Valley, sailboats, Swim Beach, foothills views
Facilities:	Restrooms, swim beach, camping

My pulse does not quicken at the prospect of flinging a catamaran across a former short-grass prairie. As a "New Westerner," I view the region's water projects as a three-card monte trick played upon rivers where I would otherwise be paddling my Old Town without interference from pontoon boats.

Yet many of Colorado's thirty-seven state parks are built around recreational reservoirs packed with more "amenities" than an amusement park. (The system is a new one, dating to only about 1960.) They've got stands of shady cottonwoods, areas hospitable to heron and loons—and Autobahn-smooth bikeways. They also offer things to do for the short, juvenile people who sometimes get dragged along on bike trips. Like splash around near sandy beaches, zoom down waterslides, fly model airplanes, or ride their own bikes out of range of the 4-by-4 brigade that marauds the state's roads.

If you don't mind the noise from the jet-ski area, 5,300-acre Chatfield State Park is a good choice for a family ride. Vaguely detumescent in shape, the 1,450-acre Chatfield Reservoir is only a dozen or so miles from Denver. A smooth road makes a favorite training ride for Denver racers. An off-road, paved trail is best for in-line skaters, kids, and adults hauling trailers or kid seats. (Or wheelchairs, for that mat-

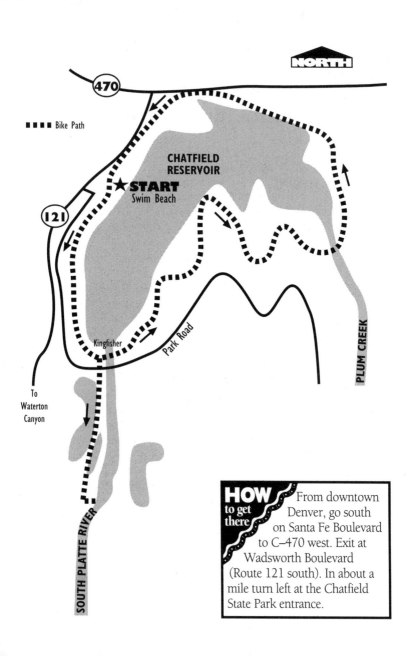

NORTH

470

■■■■ Bike Path

CHATFIELD
RESERVOIR

★ **START**
Swim Beach

121

Kingfisher

Park Road

To
Waterton
Canyon

PLUM CREEK

SOUTH PLATTE RIVER

HOW
to get
there
From downtown Denver, go south on Santa Fe Boulevard to C–470 west. Exit at Wadsworth Boulevard (Route 121 south). In about a mile turn left at the Chatfield State Park entrance.

DIREC-TIONS
at a glance

0.0   Start at Swim Beach. Turn left onto paved path heading out from parking lot.

2.0   Cross South Platte River. Turn right just before small bridge over river to explore dirt trail heading out along banks.

12.0 Return to Swim Beach.

ter. Many of the park's fishing and recreation areas are completely handicapped-accessible.)

This section of the South Platte was dammed between 1967 and 1971 after a 1965 Plum Creek flood scoured Denver to the tune of $300 million (Indians had warned the early gold-rush settlers not to build along the rivers: "Bad medicine," they said.) A fossilized mammoth skull was unearthed during excavation of a spillway in 1971.

Start at the Swim Beach near the Chatfield State Park entrance ($3.00 admission fee for a carload in 1995). Head southwest (toward the mountains) past hordes of windsurfers on your left and horse stables on your right. In about 2 miles the trail jogs left into deep woods. You cross the South Platte River just before it enters the reservoir. To see a bottomlands section of the Platte that recalls pre-dam conditions, turn right near the Kingfisher area down a dirt road that bisects a couple of lagoons. After about a mile turn left down a narrow path to reach a rocky, clear, shallow, fast section of river, perfect for swimming or wading.

Back on pavement, the trail meanders through three campgrounds and then traverses Plum Creek Nature Area, a birding spot where you're likely to see great blue herons between March and September. The magisterial birds nest in cottonwood groves before heading down to Mexico. Heading north and then west, get a good look at the earthen dam corseting the Platte. A short, swift downhill section returns you to the beach.

Fort Collins Sojourn

Distance:	13-mile loop
Approximate pedaling time:	2 hours
Terrain:	Flat
Surface:	Cement/asphalt bike path
Things to see:	Cache la Poudre River, historic downtown, nature center with captive eagles
Facilities:	Everything in downtown, playgrounds, picnic areas

I know a landscape architect who was offered a chance to start his own office in a location of his choice. After poring over maps he chose Fort Collins because of its proximity to four wilderness areas and more campgrounds than he could find clustered anywhere else.

All true, but the city's worth visiting as well. And a bike is the best way to see it.

Fifty miles north up the Front Range, Fort Collins (elevation 4,984 feet) is like Boulder without affectations. Like its neighbor, Fort Collins has about 90,000 residents, a big university (Colorado State), a red-brick downtown restored down to the last pilaster, and ribbons of paved, off-road bikeways (75 miles at this writing). And it's also a place where the bicycle has won respect as a vehicle. But in Fort Collins, you'll rarely get blown off the trail by a Cat II racer in dreadlocks. It's more likely that you'll meet families slowly cranking Huffy beach bombers toward fishing holes.

We started in downtown on a blustery October Sunday. Fort Collins has a friendly reputation and, sure enough, a shop owner came out to chat while my wife, Kathleen, and I removed bikes and trailer from the car. The silver-haired man said that he and his wife

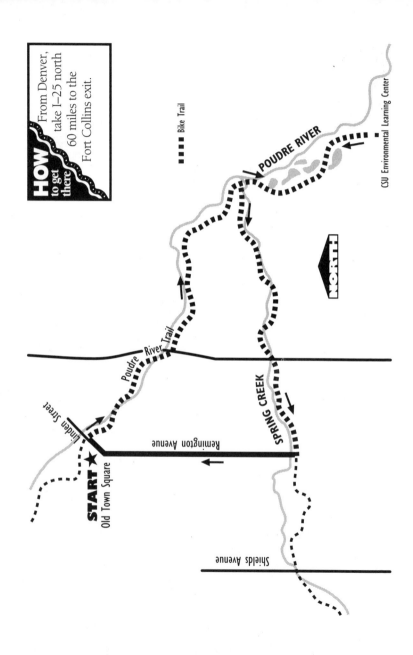

HOW to get there

From Denver, take I-25 north 60 miles to the Fort Collins exit.

Bike Trail

POUDRE RIVER

CSU Environmental Learning Center

NORTH

Poudre River Trail

SPRING CREEK

Linden Street

Remington Avenue

START
Old Town Square

Shields Avenue

DIRECTIONS at a glance

0.0 Start at Old Town Square at the corner of Linden and Walnut streets in downtown Fort Collins. Head northeast on Linden toward railroad tracks.

0.2 After crossing tracks, turn right onto Poudre River Trail.

1.6 Take right over bridge (ride on sidewalk) to stay on trail.

1.7 Go right onto trail after crossing bridge.

4.1 Go straight at intersection with Spring Creek Trail.

5.9 Arrive at CSU Environmental Learning Center. Turn around and retrace trail to Spring Creek intersection.

7.8 Turn left onto Spring Creek Trail.

11.0 Turn right onto Remington Avenue (bike lane).

13.0 Dismount at Mountain Avenue. Walk across square to ride start at Linden and Walnut.

had pedaled from Illinois to Wisconsin in the late 1940s. Their mounts were three-speed Dutch "touring bikes" with coaster brakes. "You had to brake so often that the derailleur would go out of whack every few miles," he said. "The back roads weren't very busy, but people would drive by fast and close. They weren't trying to get you, they just didn't know how to drive around bicycles." Later they started a family and kept touring; he built a bike seat himself out of plywood and aluminum.

I felt doubly lucky, for the good talk and for our lightweight, factory-built trailer as we pulled away and crossed railroad tracks toward the Cache la Poudre River (named by French traders who buried gunpowder nearby to lighten their load). The first mile is nothing special, but after you pass a golf course and cross a bridge, the river widens and the forest thickens with cottonwoods and willows. This is the greenway concept at its best. We were actually riding parallel to a busy industrial road, but the protected right-of-way made the prairie seem near, the city far.

Kingfishers dove into the Poudre as we cruised past a mini-Roebling of a suspension footbridge. At an intersection with Spring Creek, we continued straight past the sewage-treatment plant and a couple of fishing ponds to the CSU Environmental Learning Center. There a picnic meadow fronts a slatted wooden building that's home to injured birds of prey. My daughter, Nora, gaped at a golden eagle only 3 feet away. Doesn't he want to go into the forest she wondered? Yes, I answered, but his wing is broken. We walked down to the river and watched turtles poke their heads out of the water.

Returning to the Spring Creek trail, we turned left. Spring Creek itself is a verdant trickle. The path cuts past a combination of subdivisions, horse pastures, and fields of bristling grasses. We found a playground and rewarded Nora for good behavior with an hour of sliding and swinging, then headed through town on broad Remington Avenue. Fort Collins is laid out in a strict grid. Almost every street in town is as wide as a boulevard. City planners took advantage of this feature by painting wide bike lanes everywhere. They're heavily used by bikers, respected by drivers, and a great way to see the city's historic neighborhoods. Frats and sororities have taken over some of Remington's bigger houses.

We hurried down Remington to beat a gathering cloudburst. In 2 miles we were back in Old Town, sipping chilled microbrews.

For a Fort Collins Tour de Fort Bike Map, call Fort Collins Parks & Recreation at (970)221–6640.

Lory State Single-Track

Distance:	8+ miles
Approximate pedaling time:	1 hour
Terrain:	Foothills
Surface:	Gravel road, single-track dirt trails
Things to see:	Red-rock formations, reservoir
Facilities:	Restrooms, camping

Most mountain biking in Colorado is seasonal, because the best high-country trails are snowed and iced over from November to April. This is not the case at Lory State Park.

Just west of Fort Collins, the 2,400-acre park offers challenging mountain biking almost year-round. It's rare to find single-track rides this exciting, inviting, and accessible in the foothills of the Front Range.

A rugged red-rock escarpment on the park's eastern side envelops this high valley, making it feel like part of the mountains. The western ridge is more craggy, older rock: 1.7 billion years old, to be exact, topped off by the 6,790-foot landmark Arthur's Rock. Yet at 5,600 feet the valley setting has a climate more like that of Boulder or Fort Collins. There's frequent snow, yes, but lots of sunshine and warm days to keep the trails clear.

Aside from its intriguing terrain and geology, Lory State Park encompasses an ecological zone where the mountains and plains are all mixed up. This former ranch of John Howard includes short-grass prairie as well as ponderosa-pine forest. Cheatgrass, prickly pear, and yucca are scattered across the lower elevations, with mountain wildflowers like Indian paintbrush and harebells blooming at higher climes. Riders report seeing lots of wildlife, including eagles, deer, rabbits, and bear.

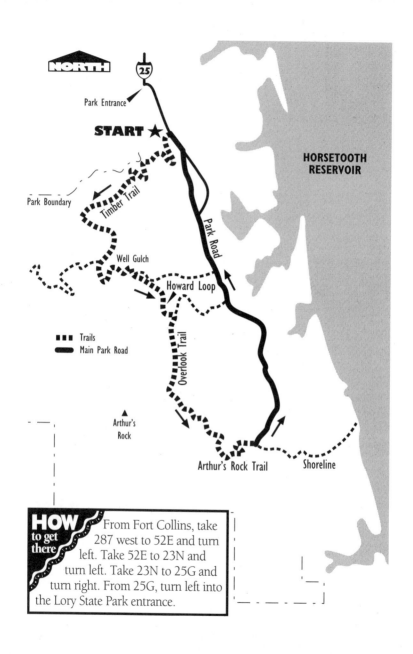

NORTH

25

Park Entrance

START ★

HORSETOOTH
RESERVOIR

Park Boundary

Timber Trail

Well Gulch

Park Road

Howard Loop

▪▪▪ Trails
━━ Main Park Road

Overlook Trail

▲
Arthur's
Rock

Arthur's Rock Trail

Shoreline

HOW
to get
there
From Fort Collins, take
287 west to 52E and turn
left. Take 52E to 23N and
turn left. Take 23N to 25G and
turn right. From 25G, turn left into
the Lory State Park entrance.

DIREC-TIONS at a glance

0.0 Start at the group picnic grounds, Timber Recreation Area. Head south on the Timber Trail.

1.7 Turn left onto Well Gulch. Timber Trail climbs sharply from here and is off-limits to bikes.

2.7 Bear right on upper Howard Loop.

3.1 Turn left onto Overlook Trail.

4.0 Turn left onto Arthur's Rock Trail.

4.2 Turn left (north) onto main park road.

8.0 Turn left into Timber Recreation Area.

Option

Two-mile round-trip on Shoreline Trail.

Lory is also a place where a multitude of recreationalists mingle. Equestrians come by the horse-trailer load, hikers in numbers, and mountain-bikers in ever-increasing packs. To some extent, each gets his own. The park includes a 320-acre cross-country jumping course. The steeper trails are reserved for hikers only. So remember mountain-biker etiquette to preserve this three-way peace: Stay on designated trails; yield to hikers and horses; downhill riders yield to those pumping uphill; respect private property; don't litter; and control your speed. Also, don't ride during or just after heavy rain or during a melt—it chews up the trails badly.

Begin this ride near the park entrance station ($3.00 admission fee in 1995) at the Timber Recreation Area. Just beyond some picnic tables, pick up the Timber Trail, a shared single-track route heading south along the western ridge. This is fairly easy and nontechnical except for a few loose, shaley sections where the trail steps up or down. Mountain biking is like downhill skiing: You should be scanning the path ahead, alert for such obstacles. If you have any doubts, get off and walk, making mental notes for the next time. Also be careful about snagging pedals on adjacent vegetation or rocks.

Bear left at an intersection with Well Gulch, an even easier section affording views of the Horsetooth Reservoir silhouetting red rock. Shortly, the trail splits again. Turn right to get onto the easy Overlook Trail, which heads due south to the lower section of Arthur's Rock Trail (the upper section is off limits to bikes). Scoot downhill to an equestrian trailhead/horse trailer parking area. From here, take an option down the 1-mile Shoreline trail to water's edge, or head back to the start on the main park road.

For more information, write Lory State Park, 708 Lodgepole Drive, Bellvue, CO 80512, or call (970) 493–1623.

Peak-to-Peak Sampler

Distance:	11 miles
Approximate pedaling time:	1 hour
Terrain:	Up-and-down mountain roads
Surface:	Paved 2-lane highway
Things to see:	Indian Peaks of the Continental Divide, historic Raymond and Riverside
Facilities:	Snacks and restroom at country store in Raymond

Running from Central City north to Estes Park, the 55-mile Peak to Peak Highway comprises some of the state's most bracing scenery, including Rocky Mountain National Park and the Indian Peaks Wilderness Area. Unfortunately, there's no easy way to fashion a short Peak-to-Peak loop. Any real circuit involves 4,000-foot climbs from the floor of Boulder Valley, too many miles and too much effort for me to recommend within the format of this "short and easy" guide.

When you feel more ambitious, every part of the highway is rideable, with excellent shoulders. Beware the southbound route from Allenspark to Ward, where the terrain rises relentlessly for about 10 miles. But if you run this section south-to-north, you can swoop down on the best views with little climbing. You might want to team up with some driving sightseers to catch a ride from the bottom.

This ride starts in the minuscule town of Raymond (elevation 7,700 feet), where a country store offers refreshment and a bathroom. Raymond was named for a family homestead that later was developed into a tiny summer resort with five cabins. The original Raymond store, a log structure with a native stone chimney, stood out behind the current store.

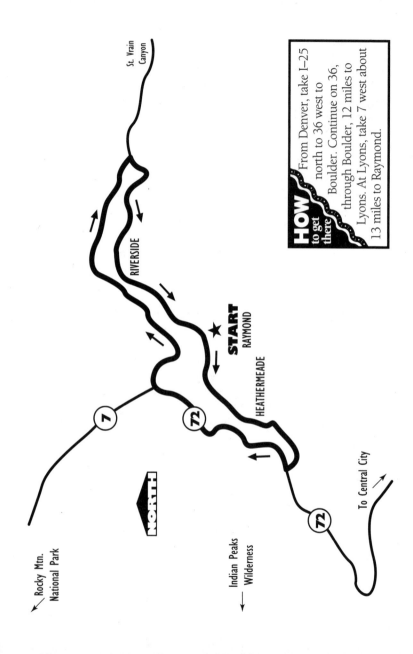

St. Vrain Canyon

RIVERSIDE

START

RAYMOND

HEATHERMEADE

7

72

72

NORTH

Rocky Mtn.
National Park

Indian Peaks
Wilderness

To Central City

HOW
to get
there

From Denver, take I-25 north to 36 west to Boulder. Continue on 36, through Boulder, 12 miles to Lyons. At Lyons, take 7 west about 13 miles to Raymond.

DIREC-TIONS at a glance

0.0 Head west from Raymond, just off the Peak to Peak Highway in Boulder County.

3.0 Turn right onto Route 72.

5.0 Turn right onto Route 7 toward Lyons.

8.0 Turn right at the sign for Riverside.

9.0 Continue west through Riverside.

11.0 Return to Raymond.

Head southwest along Middle St. Vrain Creek, lined by rustic buildings and meadows. When you hit Route 72—a section of the Peak to Peak Highway—turn right. Enjoy a several-mile downhill roll with Park Creek, the Roosevelt National Forest, and the Indian Peaks on your left, or due west.

At a T intersection, turn right onto Route 7. Follow the creek for a couple of miles as it digs into St. Vrain Canyon. Turn right at the sign for Riverside (no commercial services or restroom), several dozen weathered cabins comprising one of the state's more winsome second-home communities. Formerly the Rowley homestead, Riverside is home to one of the county's earliest cemeteries, dating from the 1870s and now an overgrown ruin. Aspens, wet meadows, and split-rail fences line the route back to Raymond.

I tested this loop as part of a much longer ride on a stormy July day. In Raymond I caught up with a group of young racers with negative body fat and $750 five-spoke wheels. I spun with them proudly for a few miles until one looked over his shoulder and tossed off, "Where are you headed, *sir*?" While I deflated faster than the Hindenburg, the bucks peeled away, effortlessly pulling on their rain gear as they cranked it up to 25 mph.

Central City Cemeteries

Distance:	8.5 miles
Approximate pedaling time:	2 hours
Terrain:	Steep climb and descent through old mining country
Surface:	Gravel and dirt roads, paved highway
Things to see:	Historic mining town and cemeteries, historic mining devastation, aspen forests
Facilities:	Hotels, opera house, Vegas-style shows, blackjack, slot machines, restaurants, restrooms all in town

Central City spans the state's extremes of landscape and culture. The first time I pumped over the Oh-My-God Road from Idaho Springs, I thought I had stumbled onto some combination of Oz and Zermatt. In a high gulch, against a mantle of pine-and-aspen mountains, honey-colored buildings embraced twisting, narrow lanes. Stone arches and elaborate cornices cast deep shadows in the alpine light. Opera-goers in evening wear scurried to the opening of *La Boheme* at the 1874 Opera House, home to a top-notch summer company.

But look again. Behind the Victorian facades (restored right down to their antique painted signs), honky-tonk gaming operations have displaced the original interiors. Twitching wagerers stumble off frog-green shuttle buses hauling bucketfuls of quarters.

Contradictions pile up even faster outside of town. One minute the ride is the Superfund special. You pass hundreds of abandoned mines. Dirt roads skim by aquamarine settling ponds. Streams reduced to rivulets of rusty water nibble through tailings piles. Jeep

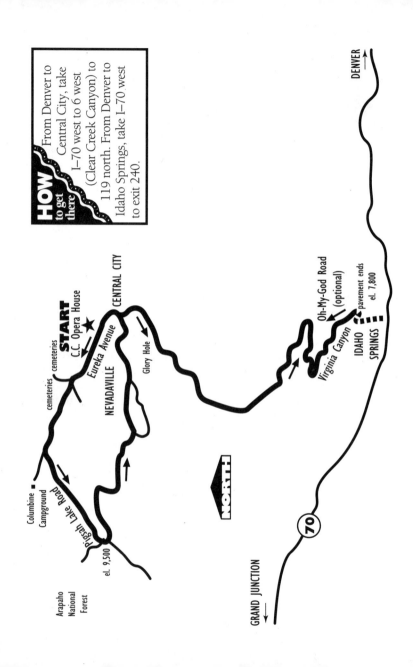

HOW to get there — From Denver to Central City, take I-70 west to 6 west (Clear Creek Canyon) to 119 north. From Denver to Idaho Springs, take I-70 west to exit 240.

DENVER

CENTRAL CITY

cemeteries   cemeteries

START
C.C. Opera House

Eureka Avenue

NEVADAVILLE

Glory Hole

Oh-My-God Road
(optional)

pavement ends
el. 7,800

Virginia Canyon

IDAHO SPRINGS

Columbine
Campground

Pisgah Lake Road

el. 9,500

Arapaho
National
Forest

NORTH

70

GRAND JUNCTION

DIREC-TIONS at a glance

0.0 Start at Opera House, on Eureka Street, Central City. Head north on Eureka and climb steadily on a paved road.

2.0 Bear left onto dirt road near Columbine Campground and bear left at each subsequent fork.

7.5 Pass through Nevadaville.

8.0 Turn left at T (279 Road).

8.5 Return to start.

Option

The Oh-My-God Road begins 1 mile north of Idaho Springs where the pavement ends on Virginia Canyon Road. The route is well signed to Central City.

roads carve up mountainsides.Climb a bit and it's a travel poster again. The aspens and gambel oak kick in, blushing during the fall like nuns at a peep show.

This ride combines jaw-dropping panoramas with the bedrock reality that Colorado was settled on the rump of activities like gold mining. And the mining was never better than around Central City, once called "the richest square mile on earth." It was the site in 1859 of Colorado's first gold-lode discovery, a source of wealth that contributed to the big-city grandeur of Central City's architecture. (The entire town is now a National Historic District.) Later the city fell on hard times. Within the past decade legal gambling—fifteen casinos featuring 3,000 slot machines, video poker, blackjack—was put in place as an economic solution. The gaming has dollars flowing again while reviving a certain vitality.

Start the ride on Eureka Avenue, in front of the Teller Opera House. These 4-foot-thick walls have hosted everyone from Edwin Booth to Lillian Gish to today's top tenors and sopranos. Heading west, climb steeply out of town toward Columbine Campground. You can't miss the ornate iron gateways to several cemeteries. Beautifully placed within the landscape, they're loaded with elaborate tombstones and paupers' grave markers alike. Stop and walk around to get a sense of the hard life of days past. Many inscriptions mention gruesome ends like explosions.

Back on the dirt road, pedal by a settling pond fringed by black plastic flapping in the wind, then a picnic area. Start climbing up switchbacks through pristine aspen groves. The ride peaks out at about 9,500 feet. You plummet into Nevadaville, a not-quite-ghost-town (population 10) once home to 1,200 souls. They were American Indians, Irish immigrants, and trained miners from Cornwall, England. Nevadaville's growth was fueled by the Glory Hole, described in *Colorado: A Guide to the Highest State* (1941) as "one of the most impressive sights in the Central City district. This great mining pit . . . is a huge rift almost 1,000 feet long and 300 feet deep in places. Shafts of old mines here were filled with dynamite and exploded, which literally blew out the heart of the mountain."

An active Masonic Lodge survives in Nevadaville. It also supports a used-book store with a good section on Colorado history. Stop in. Return to the road, come to a T, and turn left on paved blacktop for a screaming descent back into Central City.

Care for a bit more climbing through mining country? Park in Idaho Springs and twist up the Oh-My-God Road to Central City. Clinging to the side of Virginia Canyon, you gain 1,840 feet in 9 miles and pass through the semi–ghost town of Russell Gulch. Back in Idaho Springs, take the cure at the Indian Hot Springs.

Winter Park:
Single-Track Mind

Distance:	8-mile loop
Approximate pedaling time:	2 hours
Terrain:	3 short climbs within a valley
Surface:	Paved 2-lane roads, unpaved jeep roads
Things to see:	Views of the Fraser Valley, Rocky Mountain National Park, and the Indian Peaks wilderness
Facilities:	Full range in town

Though not the highest in elevation nor in the northernmost area of Colorado, Winter Park and environs are nevertheless among the state's coldest regions. That's one factor that makes the Fraser Valley, only 67 miles from Denver, a great spot for summer biking: inviting 75-degree days when the Front Range is broiling.

Winter Park was one of the first ski areas to promote its trails and roads for mountain biking. A joint effort among the U.S. Forest Service, Winter Park Resort, and Winter Park Fat Tire Society (FATS) has created more than 500 miles of mapped trails and 200 miles of signed trails. Crisscrossing the Fraser Valley, they incorporate old logging roads and routes forged by the Denver Water Board.

Many are difficult single-track trails. This one, a loop around Little/Big Vasquez Creek mapped by FATS, is not. In fact, it's a great place to try "technical" mountain biking for the first time. Many shops in town rent bikes.

Start in the town of Winter Park, whose après-ski sprawl belies the fact that it has only 586 permanent residents. The town was originally called West Portal, when it was a construction camp for the Moffat Tunnel, the Continental Divide underpass that reduced the

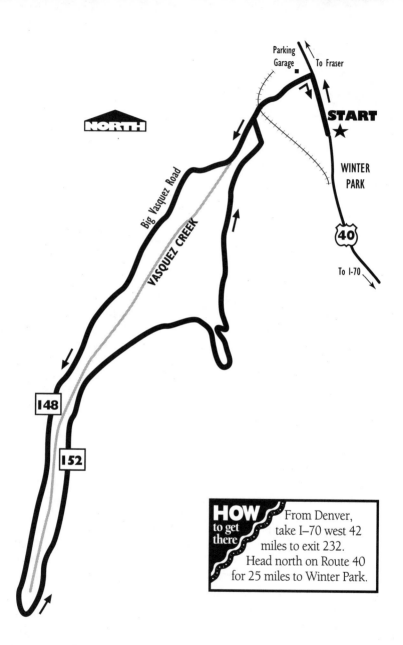

NORTH

Parking Garage

To Fraser

START

WINTER PARK

40

To I-70

Big Vasquez Road

VASQUEZ CREEK

148

152

HOW to get there
From Denver, take I–70 west 42 miles to exit 232. Head north on Route 40 for 25 miles to Winter Park.

DIREC-TIONS at a glance

0.0 Start in the Winter Park business district.
0.1 Go west on Big Vasquez Road.
0.2 Cross railroad tracks.
3.0 Big Vasquez becomes Road 148.
4.0 Make a U-turn at dam. Head back toward town on Road 152.
6.0 After crossing Little Vasquez Creek, turn left onto Little Vasquez mountain-bike trail.
7.0 Pick up Arapaho Road (paved).
7.5 Turn right onto Big Vasquez Road.
8.0 Return to start.

trip to Salt Lake City by 175 miles when completed in 1927. The Moffat also brought the first ski tourists, who used a tow rope as a ski "lift."

Start the ride (at an elevation of 8,600 feet) from one of the limitless number of parking lots in the business district along Route 40. From this bustling but charmless town center, head west on Vasquez Road past a large parking garage and a small subdivision. The pavement soon turns to packed dirt. In about a mile bear right at a fork onto Big Vasquez Road parallel to Vasquez Creek (named for explorer Zebulon Pike's interpreter). You're entering prime moose habitat within Arapaho National Forest. The continent's largest hoofed ungulate was reintroduced and now thrives in Colorado. Views to the north, east, and south are of the Continental Divide as it snakes around Fraser Valley.

Vasquez Road becomes Road 148, paralleling wildflower meadows, willow thickets, and dense forest. The route takes a 180-degree turn at a diversion dam, the ride's apogee at about 9,500 feet. Cross Vasquez Creek and head back toward town on Route 152, a short descent down a curving road. After crossing Little Vasquez Creek, turn left onto the Little Vasquez trail, a jeep road where you have to dodge a few rocks and logs. The trail passes under a large pipe carrying

water to Denver. Descend through meadows back to paved Arapaho Road. At a T intersection, turn right on Vasquez Road to return to town.

I did the ride on a 70-degree July day, serenaded by hummingbirds and Stellar's jays; back in Boulder, it was 95. I saw plenty of kids doing this ride on mountain bikes. It's too rough to tow along infants or toddlers. A better trip for the younger set is the new 5-mile Fraser River Trail connecting Winter Park with adjacent towns. A hard-packed dirt trail with little elevation change, it starts south of Winter Park and continues to the town of Fraser adjacent to Route 40. For information, contact the Winter Park/Fraser Valley Chamber of Commerce at (970) 726–4118.

Snow Mountain Figure-8

Distance:	10-mile figure-8
Approximate pedaling time:	2 hours
Terrain:	Modest up-and-down within a valley
Surface:	Dirt roads, single- and double-track mountain-bike trails
Things to see:	Views of Fraser Valley and peaks of Continental Divide
Facilities:	Lodging, restaurants, restrooms, gift shops at main lodge, bike rentals

Snow Mountain Ranch bills itself as America's family-reunion head-quarters. This is a bad hangout to pick if you like to combine day rides with all-night technoraves, or if you eschew contact with hymn-singing members of the Dodge Caravan set. But it's a great ride if you're a novice mountain cyclist seeking to combine views of moun-tain ridges with smooth riding.

Located about 80 miles west of Denver, the ranch is run by the YMCA of the Rockies as a conference center and family resort. In the mid-1960s the Y bought the property from two homesteading families, the Justs and the Rowleys. Weathered-wood ranch buildings still dot the 860 acres of the Fraser Valley, at more than 8,000 feet in elevation. A 25-mile network of trails (originally struck for Nordic skiing) am-bles through pine forests and across dogwood and willow meadows.

Summer months are cool, clear, and green. If you're not a guest at the lodge or one of its rental cabins, you can buy a trail pass for $3.00. Park at the Pinebrook Lodge administration building, an L-shaped, shingled structure about 2 miles off Highway 40. Mountain-bike rentals are available directly across the road. After buying your pass at the front desk, turn left out of the parking lot down a hard-

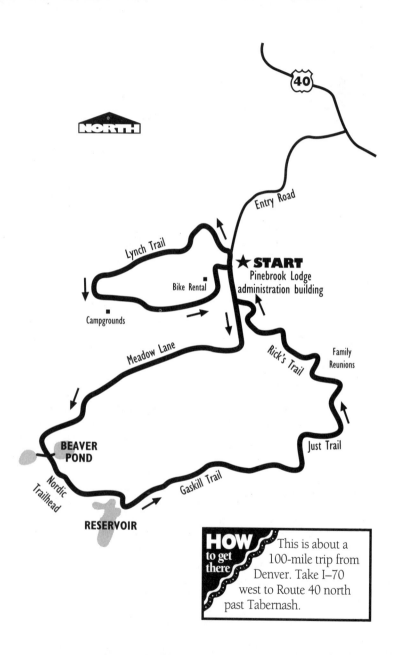

NORTH

40

Entry Road

Lynch Trail

★ **START**
Pinebrook Lodge
administration building

Bike Rental

Campgrounds

Meadow Lane

Rick's Trail

Family
Reunions

BEAVER
POND

Just Trail

Nordic
Trailhead

Gaskill Trail

RESERVOIR

HOW
to get
there
This is about a
100-mile trip from
Denver. Take I–70
west to Route 40 north
past Tabernash.

DIREC-TIONS at a glance

0.0 Start at the Pinebrook Lodge administration building. Head south on the main road.
0.5 Turn right onto Meadow Lane.
1.5 Bear left at fork.
2.1 Turn left at Snow Mountain Trailhead onto the Gaskill Trail (single-track).
4.0 Turn left onto the Just Trail (single-track).
5.0 Turn left at family-reunion area onto Rick's Bike Trail (single-track).
6.0 Turn right onto Main Road.
6.5 After passing lodge/administration building, turn left on Lynch Trail (single-track).
8.5 Cross Association Drive to remain on Lynch Trail.
9.9 Turn right onto Association Drive (mountain-bike rental on left).
10.0 Return to lodge/administration building.

packed road. In about half a mile, turn right at a three-way intersection. Turn left on Meadow Lane, a downhill roll past a livery stable, aspen stands, and some beaver ponds. After jogging around the ponds, turn left on the Gaskill Trail, your first Nordic-trail connection. Wind around a reservoir and then begin a gradual climb through aspens. Emerge in a broad meadow bisected by Pole Creek.

Follow the creek for a few miles, peeking in and out of meadows and glens and past a biathlon course. The distant view combines crystalline peaks with the rather jarring emerald green of the adjacent Pole Creek Golf Course. Turn left on Just Trail and left again at the family-reunion area. Pick up Rick's Bike Trail back to the Pinebrook Lodge, but keep going straight past the lodge and turn left onto the Lynch Trail. The trail keeps close to piney forest, and slender stumps make this ride portion a bit more technically challenging. At the Nine-Mile Trailhead, bear left to complete this loop back to the start.

For more information on mountain biking here, call Snow Mountain Ranch at (970) 887–2152 (in Denver, call 443–4743).

Ski Town Triad

Distance:	10.5 miles one way; options to Keystone and Copper Mountain
Approximate pedaling time:	2 hours
Terrain:	Flat river valley
Surface:	Top-notch paved and striped bike path
Things to see:	Mountain views, Arapaho National Forest, two historic ski towns
Facilities:	Restrooms at Frisco trailhead, all facilities in towns

You see all kinds on this ride: camel-backed racers, kids on trikes, goofy teens in Doc Martens and baggy shorts, novice riders huffing and weaving beneath lopsided rental helmets. Thanks to cool summer weather and an excellent network of off-road, paved trails, the ski towns of centrally located, peak-laden Summit County are attracting as many summer bikers as winter skiers.

Start at a parking lot and trailhead immediately off Interstate 70 at Frisco. This Victorian town once served as a rail link between Leadville and Georgetown. In the town center at 120 Main Street, Frisco Historic Park shows off seven restored buildings, including the old jail and a schoolhouse museum.

Head south on the paved Blue River Trail through forests, ponds, and along the edge of Dillon Reservoir, a popular place for sailing and a great spot to bag rainbow trout in spring. The path winds and dips until it straightens out to parallel busy Highway 9. Now you can see condos, strip developments, and whizzing cars, but you're probably paying more mind to a vista of 11,000-foot passes on the Continental Divide.

Soon you're in Breckenridge, the heart of a quartet of ski areas and

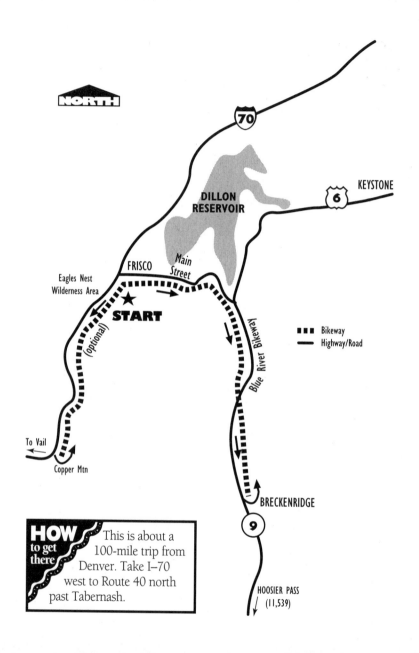

NORTH

70

KEYSTONE

6

DILLON
RESERVOIR

FRISCO

Main
Street

Eagles Nest
Wilderness Area

★ START

(optional)

Blue River Bikeway

▪▪▪ Bikeway
━━━ Highway/Road

To Vail

Copper Mtn

BRECKENRIDGE

9

HOOSIER PASS
(11,539)

HOW
to get
there

This is about a
100-mile trip from
Denver. Take I–70
west to Route 40 north
past Tabernash.

DIRECTIONS at a glance

0.0 Start at intersection of I–70 and Main Street of Frisco.

3.6 Caution: Road crossing of brief section of Frontage Road before trail resumes.

6.1 Road crossing. Trail picks up parallel to Blue River to head into town.

10.5 Arrive in downtown Breckenridge. Retrace steps to Frisco.

21.0 Return to Frisco.

Option

From Frisco trailhead, head west for six miles to Copper Mountain.

big-city busy despite its small population. Named for James Buchanan's vice president, who later joined the Confederacy as secretary of war (prompting outraged town leaders to change their town's spelling), Breckenridge was once enveloped by precious-metals mining. In 1897 the area yielded a gold nugget that weighed almost as much as a racing bike: thirteen pounds. Today the town's restored gingerbread houses seem locked in an urban design battle with condos and mini-malls. Take a slower pace by touring historic houses in eight blocks between Main, High, and Washington streets and Wellington Road.

Back at Frisco, an optional ride awaits. From the parking lot, head southwest on the Ten Mile Canyon Trail, a 6-mile route (one way) to Copper Mountain and back. Running along Interstate 70, the trail skirts south of the Eagles Nest Wilderness Area (off limits to bikes, as are all wilderness areas) and the towering Gore Range. You can take this trail all the way to Vail, but it's a very tough climb with switchbacks.

Summit County is constantly updating its bike-trail master plan. In the next few years, new routes will open to Keystone and Leadville, while the Blue River Trail will be rebuilt to avoid two dangerous road crossings. When in town, check with a local shop to get the latest, or call the Summit County Chamber at (970) 668–5800.

Pueblo Reservoir and Greenway:
The Arkansas Traveler

Distance: 26+ miles
Approximate pedaling time: 3 hours
Terrain: Flat river valley
Surface: Paved (mostly) bike path
Things to see: Recreational reservoir, nature center, bird-of-prey rehabilitation center, historic architecture, cottonwood-lined river bottoms, "world's largest mural"
Facilities: Restrooms at state park, nature center, and city park; zoo; restaurant, rafting, and bike rentals at nature center; fishing areas near Swim Lake Beach and Runyon's Crossing; parking and restrooms at Pueblo Mall

The southeastern river town of Pueblo (population 98,000) evolved as a mini-Pittsburgh of the West. Originally a trading post, the city revved up in the nineteenth century as a center for heavy manufacturing. In *Preserving the Great Plains and Rocky Mountains*, author Elaine Freed describes "a smokestack esthetic of faded red-brick . . . and grimy railroad structures, slag heaps and railroad yards."

Like many a mill town back east, however, Pueblo's fortunes began to rise as its heavy industries rusted away. A gritty charm emerged from the lifting haze. Today Pueblo is considered a highly livable city. Cleaner manufacturers moved in, and the city began to develop recreational facilities, taking advantage of its Arkansas River setting looking out at the Wet Mountains.

In the early 1970s completion of a long-planned dam created

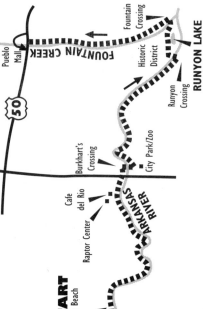

NORTH

Pueblo Mall

50

FOUNTAIN CREEK

Fountain Crossing

Historic District

RUNYON LAKE

Runyon Crossing

Burkhart's Crossing

City Park/Zoo

Cafe del Rio

Raptor Center

ARKANSAS RIVER

START

Swim Beach

(option)

dam

Bike Trail

LAKE PUEBLO

campgrounds

HOW to get there

From Denver, drive 110 miles south on I-25. To get to Lake Pueblo, head west on Route 50 for about 5 miles to Route 45. Turn left. In about 3 miles turn right into the Lake Pueblo State Park.

DIREC-TIONS at a glance

0.0 Start at Swim Lake Beach at east end of Lake Pueblo.

0.0 Head south on paved bike trail.

0.1 At T intersection of trail, turn left to head east along Arkansas River.

3.0 Arrive at Pueblo Greenway and Nature Center.

Option

Go up hill for a few hundred feet to Raptor Center.

4.0 Go right over Burkhardt's Crossing bridge.

Option

Visit City Park/Zoo. Trail continues east on south side of river.

10.0 Go left over Runyon Crossing bridge to Fountain Creek Trail through central Pueblo.

13.0 Trail ends near Route 50 and Pueblo Mall. Retrace route to start.

26.0 Return to start.

Option

Head west to explore 16.5 miles of trails around Lake Pueblo.

"Lake" Pueblo among limestone cliffs. Lake Pueblo State Park (elevation 4,900 feet) became Pueblo's first big tourist attraction. The Arkansas River (the former border between Mexican and U.S. territories) is another. Crashing out of spectacular gorges to the north, the Ark provides a popular flat-water float through this region before trundling on to Oklahoma, Little Rock, and the Mississippi River.

The long version of this ride combines two connected trails. After looping around part of the reservoir (not all of it—there are 60 miles of shoreline), a paved, off-road trail continues east along the Arkansas by fairly pristine river bottoms before delivering you to the heart of town. Most of it is a perfect family ride.

Start near Swim Lake Beach, the reservoir's swimming area, which features a sand beach and giant waterslide. Head out of the parking lot on a two-lane access road and turn left (east) at the bike path. This will lead to the 20-mile Pueblo Greenway. The trail winds around a couple of fishing ponds and parallels the Arkansas where the river is unleashed from the reservoir. It's a section of prairie river shaded by a mass of cottonwoods. Continue east for about 5 miles to a complex that includes a nature center and restaurant. Stop to enjoy the food, playground, shade, and wildflower garden. The Cafe del Rio is a convincing replica of an adobe pueblo.

Just up the hill, the Raptor Center provides shelter and nurturing for injured birds of prey. The center rehabilitates and releases injured birds when possible; otherwise they are used for educational exhibits. When I visited, this one-story building was stocked with thirty birds, including owls, hawks, kites, and a pair of bald eagles.

Back on the trail and rolling toward Pueblo, the trail takes on a hard-edged character. A 1921 flood swept away 600 houses and killed about 100 people; in 1924 the Arkansas was punished for this misdeed by being diverted and encased in massive concrete levees.

These days we try not to abuse our waterways so; in an attempt of at least cosmetic atonement, Pueblo has created the "world's largest mural." It's actually a patchwork of squares, varying wildly in quality, each created by different "artists." The pieces range from Indian patterns to images of Garfield.

Once in town, two river crossings take you near the city's heart along Fountain Creek. Connections are planned along the former riverbed that will make an easy link to the Union Avenue Historic District, home to eighty-seven Victorian-era buildings, built when Pueblo rivaled Denver as the state's largest city. The ride terminus is at Route 50. Retrace your steps to the fishing area. Once back at the start, you have the option of touring the reservoir on 16.5 miles of bike paths connecting Rock Canyon, two marinas, and campgrounds. The terrain is gorgeous: chalky limestone cliffs, blooming, spiky yuccas, and the Chinese-red blossoms of walking-stick cacti against a backdrop of indigo mountains.

I did the Pueblo Greenway ride alone on a mountain bike on a hot summer day. Near town I found part of the trail needing repair, including muddy sections and one boardwalk with missing and loose planks. Still, road bikes and rollerblades are fine for most of the length, as are bike trailers and kids on bikes. The reservoir path is kept in perfect trim.

Midland Railway Rambler

Distance:	19.3 miles
Approximate pedaling time:	3 hours
Terrain:	Mostly flat
Surface:	Hard-packed dirt road, 1 mile of single-track, gravel county roads
Things to see:	Presidential Range, Arkansas River, railroad remains
Facilities:	Showers, restrooms, drinking water at Buena Vista River Park

Buena Vista (elevation 7,800 feet) is a friendly river, mining, and railroad town in the Arkansas Valley. ("Just call us Be-yoo-nee," said the woman in the historical museum when I inquired about the preferred local pronunciation.) Though the Arkansas River draws at least 100,000 rafters and kayakers a year and the adjacent Collegiate Peaks are some of the state's highest and grandest, the town is surprisingly free of tourist-trap attitude. There's only one traffic light, and motels outnumber B&Bs by about fifty to one. The red-brick historic downtown is uncrowded and practically boutique-free.

This ride takes in the valley's best views along with some railroad history. Start at Buena Vista River Park, where you can park and watch boaters steel themselves for the Class III–IV rapids ahead. Cross the river on a wood-and-steel hiker/biker bridge, and start climbing a single-track trail among granite boulders. Relax—this is by far the toughest portion of the ride, and you can walk it easily and quickly if you need to. In about a mile turn left at an interpretive sign to follow an old railroad bed, converted to a bikeway in 1990 with the help of the U.S. Forest Service and local volunteers.

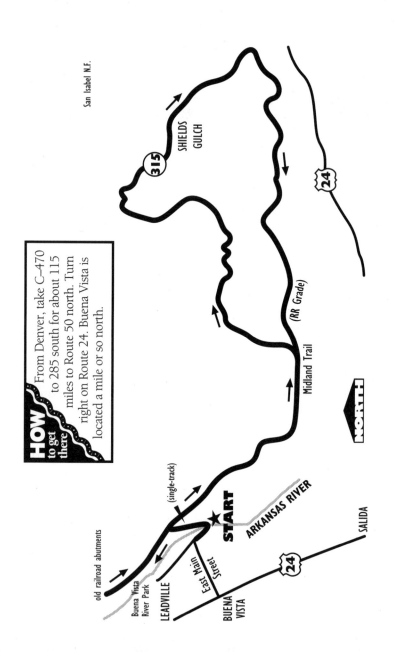

HOW to get there

From Denver, take C–470 to 285 south for about 115 miles to Route 50 north. Turn right on Route 24. Buena Vista is located a mile or so north.

San Isabel N.F.

315

SHIELDS GULCH

(RR Grade)

Midland Trail

24

NORTH

(single-track)

old railroad abutments

Buena Vista River Park

LEADVILLE

START

ARKANSAS RIVER

East Main Street

BUENA VISTA

24

SALIDA

DIREC-TIONS at a glance

0.0	Start at Buena Vista River Park at the end of East Main Street.
0.1	Cross bridge over Arkansas River. Begin climb on single-track.
1.1	Turn left at intersection onto smooth dirt road (former railroad right-of-way).
2.1	Trail dead-ends at ruin of train trestle. Turn around.
5.6	Turn left at intersection with Route 304.
6.8	Go through gate.
9.4	Turn right onto Route 315 (Shields Gulch).
11.7	Turn right onto old railbed.
13.6	Go through gate.
18.1	Turn left onto single-track.
19.1	Return to Buena Vista River Park.

The Midland Route formerly followed the river over Trout Pass to Leadville. The first standard-gauge line to cross the Continental Divide, it was out of business by 1918.

In another mile the bike trail dead-ends at the stone footings of a former trestle (dismantled for scrap iron during World War II, according to the "engineer" at the town museum's model railway).

Now turn around and double back to run the rest of the trail. The route is smooth-packed dirt, with a few sandy sections. Cars aren't banned, and you may encounter just a few. The main peaks visible across the valley are mounts Harvard (14,383 feet), Princeton (14,199 feet) and Yale (14,101 feet); all told, the region embraces more 14ers than anywhere else. The town also appears in the distance as if drawn on a plan. A promotional flyer written when the town was ten years old brags about this location "in a broad, fertile valley . . . The climate has not its superior . . . As a health resort, Buena Vista is gradually receiving the rich merit it deserves . . . a panacea for the majority of the ills of the flesh." (This embroidery, by the way, is printed right above an etching of a vast, belching paper mill.)

The trail passes through low canyons blasted out when the railroad came through. Vegetation is scrubby piñon pine and rabbitbrush. About halfway through the ride, you start climbing gradually before a fast descent on a sandy section down Shields Gulch. A few more single-track detours are necessary to go around abandoned trestles (these originally crossed four "draws"—Coloradan for drainages). Then it's back to smooth dirt and the River Park. The valley doesn't get a lot of snow despite its high elevation. This ride's a good bet all year round.

Buena Vista and environs are catching on to the virtues of mountain biking for all skill levels. A group called the Banana Belt Fat Tracks promotes the sport and publishes a trail guide. For more information, call the Otero Cyclery in Salida at (719) 539–6704.

Peregrination to Princeton Hot Springs

Distance:	10.2 miles
Approximate pedaling time:	1 hour
Terrain:	Steep climb followed by rapid descent
Surface:	2-lane blacktop, dirt road, short single-track
Things to see:	Chalk Valley, waterfalls, hot springs
Facilities:	Hot-springs resort, including restaurant and lounge, campground

Here's a ride that offers a bit of everything: a ride up the geologically unique Chalk River Valley, a touch of single-track, a smooth glide down two-lane blacktop, a hike up to some misty falls, and soothing hot springs when it's all over.

Start at the Princeton Hot Springs, just a few miles south of Buena Vista and adjacent to the tiny town of Nathrop (named for pioneer merchant Charles Nachtrieb, who was murdered here in 1881) and to San Isabel National Forest. Dating back to bathhouses built in the 1870s, this hot-springs resort features more than twenty spots to take a dip. They range from hot tubs to rock pools built by pilgrims attending the Harmonic Convergence in 1987. Temperatures vary from tolerably cool to unbearably hot. Admission was $6.00 in 1995.

But save the bathing for last. Head out of the parking area west on Route 162 into the National Forest. Chalk Creek is at the left, the chalky-white rock formations of the Sawatch Range to the right. These eroded rocks are not chalk but kaolinite, a soft rock formed by leaching from hot water rising among the faults that line the valley.

Lock up opposite the seventeen-site Mount Princeton Campground for a half-mile hike up Cascade Falls, a verdant escape from

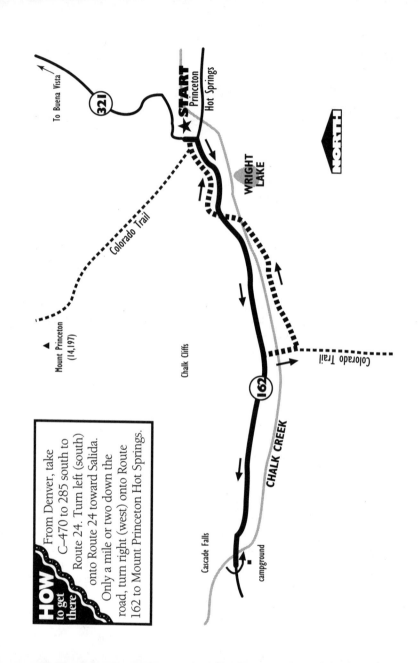

HOW to get there From Denver, take C-470 to 285 south to Route 24. Turn left (south) onto Route 24 toward Salida. Only a mile or two down the road, turn right (west) onto Route 162 to Mount Princeton Hot Springs.

To Buena Vista

321

★ START
Princeton
Hot Springs

WRIGHT LAKE

Colorado Trail

Mount Princeton (14,197)

Chalk Cliffs

162

Colorado Trail

CHALK CREEK

Cascade Falls

campground

NORTH

DIRECTIONS at a glance

0.0 Start at Princeton Hot Springs, Route 162, Nathrop.

0.1 Turn left out of parking area onto 162.

5.1 Arrive at Mount Princeton Campground/ Cascade Falls. Hike the falls and turn around, heading east on 162.

7.2 Turn right onto Colorado Trail trailhead.

7.5 Turn left onto smooth dirt road.

9.2 Turn right onto Route 162 east.

10.2 Return to Princeton Hot Springs.

---

otherwise spare surroundings. (Note: No bikes are allowed on this trail.) After your hike, double back down Route 162 for about 2 miles and turn right into the Colorado Trail trailhead. The first ⅓ mile is single-track through a scrubby pine-and-paintbrush landscape—easy stuff except for the first brief, boulder-strewn climb. Then it's left on a dirt road (still part of the Colorado Trail) overlooking Chalk Creek.

At a Y fork, pick up Route 162 again and sail back down to Princeton Hot Springs. The grade is fairly steep. I clocked only about 8 mph heading uphill toward the falls but nearly 30 mph heading back down.

If you want to bike from Princeton to Buena Vista, don't follow the main drag. Take the quiet 321 Road through ranchland due north to Cottonwood Pass Road. Turn right and proceed to Main Street.

The Arkansas Valley communities are catching on to the virtues of mountain biking for all skill levels. A group called the Banana Belt Fat Tracks promotes the sport and publishes a trail guide. For more information, call the Otero Cyclery in Salida at (719) 539–6704.

Glenwood Canyon:
Riding the Interstate

Distance:	16.3 miles one way
Approximate pedaling time:	3 hours
Terrain:	600-foot drop (and gain) in elevation
Surface:	Paved bike path
Things to see:	Historic town with hot-springs baths, spectacular canyon scenery, section of Colorado River, historic power station
Facilities:	Hotels, restaurants, restrooms

Before the era of prescription drugs, people seeking balms "took the waters" at hot springs. Glenwood Springs (elevation 5,763 feet) became a premiere destination, thanks to its proximity to lots of mineral springs flowing from limestone formations. Located between the Flat Top Mountains and a dramatic canyon at the confluence of the Colorado and Roaring Fork rivers, the city developed in the 1880s with large, grand resort hotels. The town center holds the world's largest hot-springs pool, a brick-lined wonder measuring 75 by 615 feet. Originally called Defiance, after a fort a few miles away, the town was later renamed for Glenwood, Iowa, the birthplace of one of its founders.

The golden age of spas has passed, but Glenwood's red-brick architecture and hot-springs pools are intact. Excursion trains from Denver and adjacent Interstate 70 corral a steady flow of tourists.

Glenwood is also base camp for a marvelous new bike path: a 16.3-mile paved trail that runs parallel to the interstate. Here the canyon embraces a veritable ganglion of transportation. You'll see scores of rafters plying a bumpy section of the Colorado, freight trains and Amtrak superliners across the river on tracks blasted by the D&RG in 1887, and lots of drivers speeding by on Interstate 70.

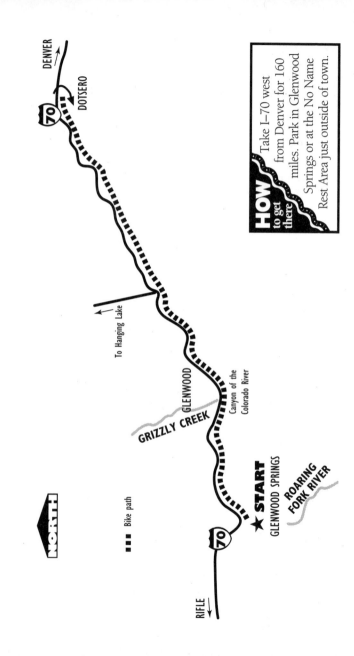

NORTH

DENVER

DOTSERO

70

To Hanging Lake

GLENWOOD

Canyon of the
Colorado River

GRIZZLY CREEK

■ ■ ■ Bike path

★ START
GLENWOOD SPRINGS

ROARING
FORK RIVER

70

RIFLE

HOW to get there — Take I–70 west from Denver for 160 miles. Park in Glenwood Springs or at the No Name Rest Area just outside of town.

DIREC-TIONS at a glance

0.0 Start in downtown Glenwood Springs. Head east on Sixth Street.

0.5 Turn left over a highway overpass bridge to bike trail.

1.8 No Name Rest Area.

3.8 Grizzly Creek Rest Area.

7.8 Hanging Lake trailhead.

12.8 Bair Ranch Rest Area.

16.3 End of trail at Dotsero. Retrace steps to start.

Begin the ride in the town center, near the pool. Head east on Sixth Street and go past the Yampah Vapor Caves, another geothermal wonder, first used by the Ute Indians for therapeutic purposes. Today the caves are heated to 115 degrees. You can get a facial or a foot massage on the return trip.

As you near the caves, follow signs that lead to a paved bike path that runs parallel to Interstate 70. Riding a bike next to an interstate may not sound so pleasant, but this is a great family ride, easy pedaling with amazing scenery. Here's how *Colorado: A Guide to the Highest State* described the setting in 1941:

> The highway swings southwest between slate-colored cliffs as it follows the valley of the Colorado to the mouth of the Glenwood Canyon, trenched through sedimentary rock and underlying granite for 15 miles, one of the outstanding scenic attractions of Colorado. Sheer walls here and there rise 1,000 feet above the foaming river as it cascades down a series of rapids. Throughout the canyon are alternate bands of limestone, granite, and red sandstone. High on the serrated walls pine trees cling precariously.

When that passage was prepared, State Road 6 snaked through the canyon. By the 1970s Glenwood Canyon had become a missing link in the Interstate 70 route. Mounting pressure to build a modern highway was met by avid opposition. It took an act of the U.S. Congress to forge a compromise. The highway would be built, but the Colorado Department of Transportation would take unheard-of measures to mitigate or repair damage from construction.

To minimize the effects upon White River National Forest, much of the road rides 30 feet *above* the river on concrete piers. Rock faces that had to be blasted were stained to match the natural cliffs. More than 180,000 greenhouse-raised native plants, including gambel oak and sagebrush, were plunked into the ground. The roadbuilders also had to proffer plenty of recreation: seventy-four scenic pull-outs, access ramps for whitewater rafts, and this state-of-the-art bikeway.

Worthwhile pauses along the way include the No Name Rest Stop, a good place to observe bighorn sheep ambling over the canyon's Precambrian rock. Located midway through the trail, Grizzly Creek Rest Area has bike racks if you care to lock up and hike along the creek. The river roars out of a 2.7-mile tunnel into furious rapids near the historic Shoshone Power Station.

Hanging Lake, a terrific hiking trail, is one of the state's most photographed spots. Formed by a fault below the valley floor, the searing-blue lake is fed by waterfalls. It's a climb, 930 feet up a side canyon. The bike trail ends in the town of Dotsero, supposedly named for Dot Zero, the surveying baseline for the Denver & Rio Grande Railway.

I rode Glenwood Canyon on a hot Labor Day. I was on a mountain bike, but road bikes are more appropriate. In-line skaters and kids find this route easy and enjoyable. It's safe for hauling a bike trailer or child seat.

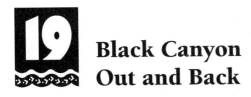

Black Canyon
Out and Back

Distance:	16 miles round-trip
Approximate pedaling time:	2 hours
Terrain:	Canyon rim with rolling topography
Surface:	Narrow, paved 2-lane road
Things to see:	Views of a canyon that's ½-mile deep but only 40 feet wide in places
Facilities:	Campgrounds and restrooms in park; all other services in nearby communities

The Black Canyon is the Rockies in reverse. Buried among endless, spare mesas, the canyon is a scenic surprise that guards its secrets until you practically fall into them. "[N]o other canyon in North America combines the depth, narrowness, sheerness, and somber countenance of the Black Canyon of the Gunnison," wrote Wallace Hansen in his book *The Black Canyon of the Gunnison: In Depth*.

Designated a National Monument and administered by the National Park Service since 1933, this mist-shrouded 12-mile stretch of the canyon is also largely protected as a wilderness area, rich with bird and bear. Not until 1901 did an engineering crew first make a successful run down the Black Canyon—33 miles in nine days. The river drops 95 feet per mile, making it one of the fastest and most treacherous waterways in America.

Cyclists can make the trip much more easily on smooth rim roads. The route follows the standard driving tour, but it's much better done on a bike. You'll want to stop often and won't have to mess with parking. Rangers at the visitor center assured me that despite the narrow road, they hadn't lost any cyclists lately. However, the lack of shoulders would make me think twice before taking kids along. I left mine behind.

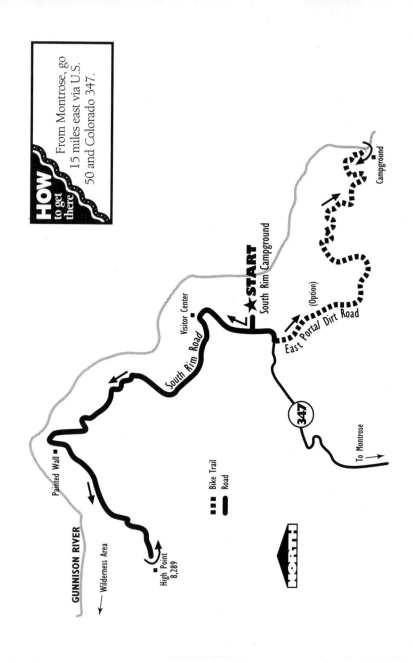

HOW to get there

From Montrose, go 15 miles east via U.S. 50 and Colorado 347.

Campground

START
South Rim Campground

East Portal/ Dirt Road
(Option)

Visitor Center

South Rim Road

347

To Montrose

Painted Wall

GUNNISON RIVER

Wilderness Area

High Point
8,289

Bike Trail
Road

NORTH

DIREC-TIONS
at a glance

0.0 Start at South Rim Campground. Head north.

8.0 Arrive at High Point. Turn around.

16.0 Return to South Rim Campground.

Option

0.0 From South Rim Campground, head south.

0.5 Go left on East Portal Road.

5.0 Arrive at East Portal Dam. Turn around.

10.0 Return to South Rim Campground.

Start at the South Rim Campground (elevation 8,320 feet) with campsites nuzzled into a scrub-oak forest. Head north on the South Rim Road. The first canyon views unfold at Gunnison Point (elevation 8,150 feet), a few miles up the road. Stop in at the visitor center and take the time to walk the 750 feet to the overlook for a view of the canyon's North Wall. It's a solid Precambrian wall, about 1.7 billion years old—some of the oldest exposed rock on Earth. The river plunges 1,820 feet below. Here I overheard two apparent Christian fundamentalists discussing this particular aspect of creation. "You can't tell me," said a man in a Garth Brooks shirt, waving his hands, "that *nature* made all that!" I didn't agree with him, but I appreciated his sense of awe.

Back on the road, proceed to Pulpit Rock and walk the length of a football field to the next overlook. Here the canyon presents two distinctly different ecologies on facing walls. The south rim gets little sun and is a hard-bitten, raw talus slope. The warmer north rim wall is forested with Douglas fir.

Chasm View (7,760 feet) is the next stop: The canyon widens out to about 1,100 feet, but the river is rushing more furiously than ever, having dropped 500 feet in the last 2 miles. Start climbing again past

Painted Wall View (where a tamer river is on display) toward High Point (8,290). Time to turn around unless you care to walk the brief Warner Point Nature Trail.

Want to see the river closer up? A challenging option takes you down to the Gunnison's banks. From the South Rim Campground, head south and east another ½ mile and turn left on East Portal Road. The rough dirt road demands a mountain bike. It plunges down switchbacks about 1,800 feet to a campground at the edge of Curecanti Recreation Area, a region in which the Gunnison has been tamed through three dams. Before you undertake this parachute jump, remember that what goes down must ride back up—in this case, back up a 14 percent grade. Bring at least two water bottles and food for this 10-mile round-trip, for strong cyclists only.

This ride illustrates what some conservationists have been arguing for decades—that you don't need a car to enjoy our national parks. The Park Service has already figured this out and is looking for ways not just to allay the mounting traffic jams in parks but also to bring visitors "face-to-face with the resource," as an administrator might say. Edward Abbey proposed putting tourists on donkeys, but the mountain bike hadn't been invented then. Get away from the tape decks, the a/c, and the exhaust, and start listening to the bel canto of the canyon wren. You'll never go back.

Durango-Trimble Soak

Distance:	22 miles
Approximate pedaling time:	2–3 hours
Terrain:	Flat river valley
Surface:	2-lane blacktop, city roads, a bit of 4-lane with shoulder
Things to see:	Hot springs, historic railroad town, open country
Facilities:	Restrooms at train station, developed hot springs, tourist amenities in town

Durango is one of several towns in our bike-friendly state that can fairly lay claim to the title "Mountain-Bike Capital of. . . ." The nearby San Juans (formed by volcanoes and perhaps the state's most striking range) are full of dirt roads and single-track trails. When the area hosted the World Mountain Bike Championships, nine of the top thirty finishers were from Durango.

In the road-bike department, Durango also hosts the largest, oldest race in Colorado. Every Memorial Day weekend, some 2,000 roadies dash against a steam train (see below) for 47 miles to see who can reach Silverton first. The overall elevation gain exceeds 6,000 feet.

Durango sits at 6,500 feet within the red sandstone bluffs of the Animas River Valley. The area is officially semiarid, yet it's greener than other parts of Colorado because of warmer weather and a rain dividend from the San Juans. A magnet for Texans seeking cooler climes in summer, the area is also the gateway to Mesa Verde National Park. You may recognize the setting—*Butch Cassidy and the Sundance Kid* was filmed here in the late 1960s.

Originally a rough-hewn railroad nexus serving the mining boom,

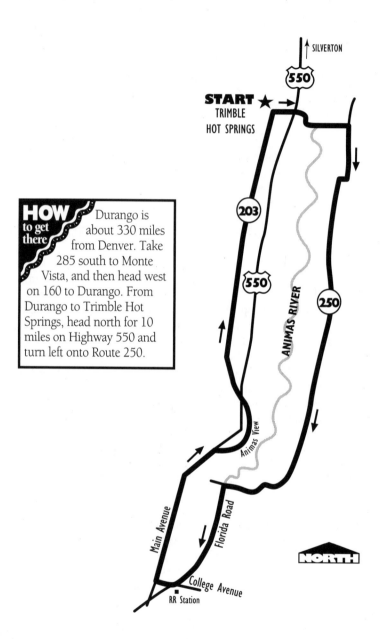

↑ SILVERTON

[550]

START ★ →
TRIMBLE
HOT SPRINGS

[203]

[550]

[250]

ANIMAS RIVER

HOW
to get
there
Durango is about 330 miles from Denver. Take 285 south to Monte Vista, and then head west on 160 to Durango. From Durango to Trimble Hot Springs, head north for 10 miles on Highway 550 and turn left onto Route 250.

Animas View

Main Avenue

Florida Road

NORTH

College Avenue

■ RR Station

DIREC-TIONS at a glance

0.0	Start at Trimble Hot Springs, just west of the intersection of Rural Route 250 and Highway 550.
0.0	Turn right out of parking lot.
0.1	Turn left onto Route 250 south.
0.2	Cross Highway 550 at light. Continue straight on Route 250.
10.0	Turn right at T intersection onto Florida Road (Route 250).
10.5	Florida Road becomes Third Avenue (historic district).
10.8	Turn left onto Seventeenth Street.
10.8	Turn right onto Main Street.
11.0	Arrive at train station. Turn around and head north on Main Street.
13.0	Turn right onto Animas View Drive.
15.0	Cross Route 550 at light to stay on Animas View Drive (Route 203).
22.0	Arrive at Trimble Hot Springs.

Durango retains much of its railroad feel, thanks to the Durango & Silverton Narrow Gauge Railroad. The 90-mile round-trip is meant for tourists (not commuters), yet it carries more passengers (200,000 a year in the May-to-October season) than some Amtrak lines. The puff of coal-fired trains is constantly evident over Durango's historic downtown.

This ride, a gentle introduction to the valley's diversions, begins 11 miles north of central Durango, at Trimble Hot Springs. Why here and not Durango? Follow this ride and you'll still see the town but look forward to bathing in a 108-degree therapy pool at journey's end. The recently revitalized resort features an Olympic-sized outdoor pool kept at 85 degrees and smaller pools maintained at 102 and 108 degrees. The setting includes gardens, a park, picnic areas, and a volleyball court. Admission in 1995 was $6.00 for adults, $4.00 for kids age 12 and under. The springs also hosts a jazz festival in July.

From the springs, cross Highway 550 and head south on Rural Route 250. You'll course through a broad valley with horse farms, pasteled mesas and plateaus, and the winding, soulful Animas River. The road runs parallel to the narrow-gauge tracks. Closer to town the scenery becomes more suburban; Durango is booming.

Once in town, ride on a marked on-street bikeway through the Third Street historic district. That leads to the downtown historic district, anchored by the red-and-white Strater Hotel of 1882. The restored train station is the people-watching spot in town. Other downtown landmarks include the funky Durango Diner and Gardenschwartz, an outdoor store-cum-taxidermy museum. Gentrification gallops through as well, personified by the Ralph Lauren and Bolle shops near the main drag.

Return by heading due north on Main Street and sloshing through a motel strip (more-than-adequate shoulders for cyclists) before busting out on Highway 550. A right turn on Animas View Drive (a former townsite) takes you deep into river bottomlands on a smooth, quiet, two-lane road. You're closer to the mountain ridge than before but still well within a vast flood plain strewn with cottonwoods and willows. Enjoy the view of houses hewn from local stone, ranches, pastures, farms, organic farms, ponds, and log houses before returning to Trimble.

Care to try some mountain biking from here? Drive north on Highway 550 about 17 miles to the Purgatory ski area. From the ski-area parking lot, ask directions to the Hermosa Creek trailhead (it's famous), a challenging 21-mile ride with a 2,000-foot elevation change. Purgatory also sells lift tickets to mountain bikers who wish to ride Nordic trails in summer.

From Durango
to Ute Country

Distance:	19 miles
Approximate pedaling time:	2 hours
Terrain:	Flat river valley
Surface:	City streets, 2-lane blacktop, hard-packed gravel road, highway shoulder
Things to see:	Quiet farmland against a mountain backdrop
Facilities:	Country store in Durango

Not far from Durango, the Anasazi Indian ruins at Mesa Verde National Park attract 700,000 visitors a year. That makes it tough for the cyclist: You've got to compete with motor-home traffic choking dusty, narrow roads. So I don't recommend a Mesa Verde ride in this book.

But there's another road that you can ride directly out of Durango to visit impressive Indian ruins visited by only *3,000* people a year. The route is a scenic, traffic-free, straight shot out of town into the Ute Mountain Tribal Park, within the Southern Ute Indian Reservation.

The only hitches: You need permission in advance and you must pay a $25 permit fee to enter the Tribal Park. (Call 970–565–3751.) "The Utes have done an excellent job of preservation," observes Patti McCarthy, a Durango publicist. The 125,000-acre park includes thousand-year-old cliff dwellings, petroglyphs, and pictographs. (To arrange a separate mountain-bike/hike tour of the park, write Mountain Bike Specialists, P.O. Box 1389PR, Durango, CO 81301, or call 970–247–4066.)

Start in town at the train station. After turning onto a busy road with strip developments, cruise downhill and bear right onto a frontage road, in front of a small industrial park. Bear right at the end

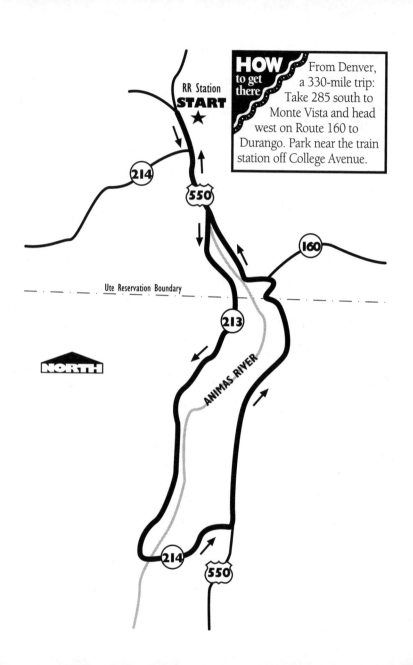

RR Station
START

HOW *to get there* From Denver, a 330-mile trip: Take 285 south to Monte Vista and head west on Route 160 to Durango. Park near the train station off College Avenue.

214

550

160

Ute Reservation Boundary

213

NORTH

ANIMAS RIVER

214

550

DIREC-TIONS at a glance

0.0 Start at train station, College and Main, downtown Durango. Head west on College for 3 blocks.

0.2 Turn left onto Route 550 south.

1.4 Bear right onto Frontage Road near industrial park.

1.8 Bear right onto Route 213.

7.0 Pavement ends; road becomes smooth dirt.

8.8 Turn left onto bridge over Animas (Route 214).

9.8 Turn left onto 550 north.

18.8 Turn right onto College Avenue in downtown Durango.

19.0 Return to start.

of the frontage road to start the scenic portion. You're following a low canyon of the Animas River, heavily fished for rainbow trout here. The Animas is one of Colorado's last free-flowing rivers. This section is supposed to make a pleasant paddle with only a few rapids.

You're only a mile and a half out of town but already deep into ranch country. The only other vehicle you'll probably see is an occasional pickup. Over your right shoulder, the road's western edge is dense with gambel oak—a sea of scarlet in autumn.

There's a gate at the border of Ute territory. You can enter only if escorted by a guide according to prior arrangement. The ride offers a chance to see the ruins of kivas and rubble dwellings in a natural setting. After completing the tour, leave the reservation via the Bondad Bridge.

After heading east for 2 miles, you'll take Route 550 north—the Million Dollar Highway, originally a nineteenth-century mining route. This is a somewhat busy road, but with an excellent shoulder. The views ahead of the San Juans are nonpareil. If you'd rather not ride the highway, retrace your steps on Route 213 to town.

I did a modified version of this ride on a perfect summer morn.

Western tanagers flitted through the piñon, and light danced on the Animas. I left at 7:00 A.M. and was back by 9:00 for breakfast at the Durango Diner on Main Street. The trip is doable on a road bike, but I don't recommend it for kids.

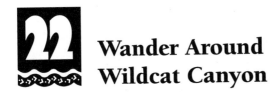

Wander Around Wildcat Canyon

Distance:	14.2 miles
Approximate pedaling time:	90 minutes
Terrain:	Hilly
Surface:	Paved and dirt roads
Things to see:	Downtown Durango, desert canyons and prairie
Facilities:	Hotels, restaurants, restrooms, etc., in downtown

Even in today's gentrified state, Durango epitomizes the ruffian West. After its founding in the 1880s, the town drew a crowd of cowhands, prospectors, miners, gamblers, and railroad construction hands. Commented *Colorado: A Guide to the Highest State:* "The notorious Stockton-Eskridge gang of desperadoes carried their warfare throughout the country, rustling cattle and jumping claims . . . A street car line ran for less than a year because the crews were abusive and insulting to patrons, and the cars invariably pulled away from the railroad station before all incoming passengers could get aboard."

This ride serves up some of that cowboy heritage, though it's largely more sedate—even deserted—today. Start at the railroad station in town. Follow the signs out of town toward Mesa Verde National Park. Route 160 west is, briefly, a six-lane artery lined by auto dealerships and starburst-neon 1950s motels. It's safe for cyclists.

At the Wildcat Canyon Lodge, turn left onto the newly paved Wildcat Canyon Road. The canyon is really a low valley, with squat buttes and cliffs lined by sagebrush and gambel oak. Houses along this route were threatened by wildfires during the epic drought/heat

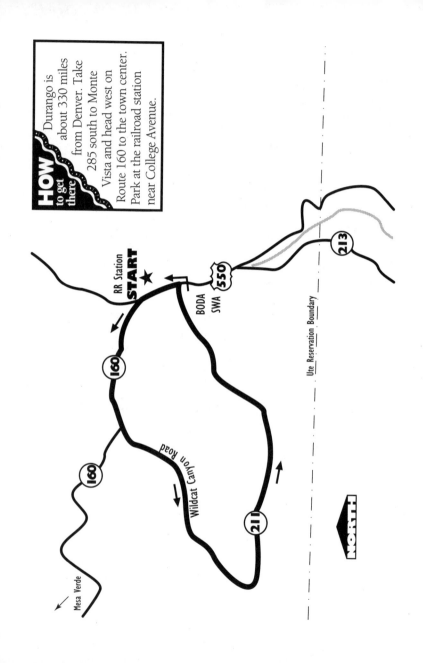

HOW to get there

Durango is about 330 miles from Denver. Take 285 south to Monte Vista and head west on Route 160 to the town center. Park at the railroad station near College Avenue.

RR Station
START

160

160

Mesa Verde

Wildcat Canyon Road

211

BODA SWA

550

213

Ute Reservation Boundary

NORTH

DIRECTIONS at a glance

0.0	Start at train station, College and Main, downtown Durango. Go west on College Avenue.
0.2	Follow signs to Mesa Verde (Route 160).
2.2	Turn left at Wildcat Lodge onto Wildcat Canyon Road.
4.7	Turn left onto Route 211.
12.2	Turn left at 550 onto Frontage Road.
14.2	Turn right onto College Avenue for return to railroad station.

wave of 1994; and residents posted THANK YOU, FIREFIGHTERS signs along their drives.

The canyon opens up with spectacular mountain views to the north. Turn left onto Route 211, a dirt road following a dry wash. Scrub cedar lines a high desert landscape as you coast slightly downhill. The next 7 miles wind through pleasantly deserted ranchland owned by the federal Bureau of Land Management. Be prepared: There's no water or services, and it can be hot on this dusty back road, which appears to be miles from nowhere. You pass abandoned ranch houses and corrals falling apart like so many pickup sticks. The end of the road becomes a canyon, with a swift, curving descent through the Bodo Wildlife Area. All told, a great way to escape the hordes in downtown Durango.

Lime Creek Blues

Distance:	21 or 24 miles
Approximate pedaling time:	3 hours
Terrain:	Steady descent down river valley and climb over Coal Bank Pass (elevation 10,600 feet)
Surface:	2-lane highway, 1- and 2-lane Jeep road
Things to see:	2,000-foot canyon, trout stream, high mountains of the San Juan range, beaver ponds
Facilities:	None

"Be sure to start this ride at the *south* end and ride from *south* to *north*," said the mechanic in a Durango bike shop. We had heard from other tourists that Lime Creek was a terrific ride, and had decided to seek some local knowledge before driving the 25 miles north from town.

Following the mechanic's directions, we parked near some stables with mules for rent, hooked up the bike trailer, and headed up the slightly rocky, unpaved road. And up. And still farther up. We climbed for 10 of the next 12 miles through an incredible gorge lined by 2,000-foot cliffs. The ride was just as splendid as billed. But it took three hours, hauling a two-year-old and assorted gear. At the end of this route, near where Lime Creek Road loops back into Highway 550, we encountered two caps-backwards college kids leading a mountain-bike tour. They were riding *toward* us. "You started at the wrong end," one said dryly. So we had deduced.

From either direction, this ride offers a pleasurable introduction to nontechnical mountain biking in San Juan National Forest, a spare and

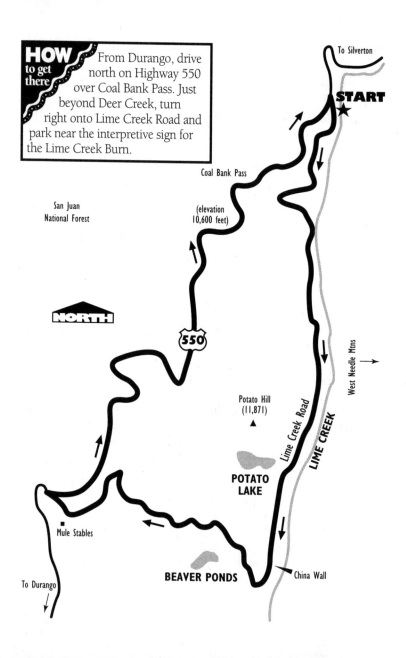

HOW to get there From Durango, drive north on Highway 550 over Coal Bank Pass. Just beyond Deer Creek, turn right onto Lime Creek Road and park near the interpretive sign for the Lime Creek Burn.

To Silverton

START

Coal Bank Pass

San Juan National Forest

(elevation 10,600 feet)

NORTH

550

Potato Hill (11,871)

Lime Creek Road

LIME CREEK

West Needle Mtns

POTATO LAKE

Mule Stables

BEAVER PONDS

China Wall

To Durango

DIREC-TIONS at a glance

0.0 Start at the northern intersection of Highway 550 and Lime Creek Road. Follow Lime Creek Road south.

12.0 Arrive at northern intersection of Highway 550 and Lime Creek Road. Turn around to retrace steps or turn right onto 550.

21.0 Arrive back at start.

stony setting worthy of a Bierstadt painting. But most people will want to begin at the *north* end, at elevation 9,650 feet, just past Deer Creek and a brown interpretive sign for the Lime Creek Burn on the right along Highway 550. Park by the sign to begin a descent into Lime Creek Canyon. What begins looking like a simple Jeep road into the Needle Mountains becomes a significant engineering feat. Much of this road was blasted out of solid Precambrian gneiss, rock that is about 1.7 billion years old. Tilled soil is a rarity in these craggy environs.

As the interpretive sign explains, the Lime Creek Burn cleared 26,000 acres of forest in 1879. Dense stands of aspens and evergreens are much in evidence today. The road rolls on down, lined by a mixed bouquet of fireweed, columbine, Indian paintbrush, and harebells. Two ashen-faced 13ers are on your left: Mount Twilight and Mount Snowden. Near Potato Lake the road meets the creek on your left. Take lunch at the comely Forest Service campground, a trout-fishing mecca where the creek features nice swimming eddies.

From this elevation of about 8,800 feet, begin a tough climb to the China Wall at 9,700 feet. The road clings precariously to rocky bluffs that diminish the creek to a far-off trickle. A stone parapet built by the Forest Service as a guard rail here doesn't offer much comfort to vertigo-sufferers.

Switchbacks beat the retreat from the wall into a broad, aspen-fringed valley teeming with beaver ponds. You can see the ski runs of the Purgatory area carved in the distance. Lime Creek Road then jogs west and downhill through an aspen forest before rejoining Route 550, near an outfitter that rents burros.

Two choices here: Either turn around to retrace your steps up Lime Creek Road (a tough climb), or proceed to the T and turn right onto Highway 550 north. The highway route vaults over Coal Bank Pass (10,600 feet) on a smooth, paved, two-lane road with a 35-mph speed limit. After a steady 6-mile climb, you might hit 45 mph on the descent. Yet another option: Pack off the car keys with a designated cyclist willing to run the shuttle.

Orvis-Ouray Orbit

Distance:	22 miles round-trip
Approximate pedaling time:	2 hours
Terrain:	700-foot climb heading toward Ouray
Surface:	Quiet, unpaved road
Things to see:	Historic town with hot-springs baths, spectacular canyon scenery, section of Uncompahgre River
Facilities:	Hotels, restaurants, restrooms in Ouray; hot springs, hot tubs, motel rooms, camping at Orvis

The mountain/mining town of Ouray (elevation 7,750 feet) is so high that people say they can only grow rhubarb in their vegetable gardens. Yet columbine sprouts like a weed in sidewalk cracks. A self-proclaimed look-alike for a Swiss hamlet, Ouray is indeed picturesque. But it is also rather noisy and dusty, due to a constant flow of Jeep tourists heading west into the Uncompahgre National Forest. Western movie buffs might recognize the valley as the setting for John Wayne's *True Grit* of 1969.

Most of this 6-by-9-block town is listed as a National Historic District. Take the walking tour before jumping on your bike. Highlights include the Western Hotel, at 220 Seventh Avenue; the onion-domed county courthouse, on Fourth Street; and Wright's Opera House at Fifth and Main. The County Museum, on Fifth Street, was originally a St. Joseph Hospital. You can visit the old operating room, still set up with scalpels, and shudder to think that it was used into the 1960s.

This ride heads east into the Uncompahgre Valley as it flattens out toward quiet mesa country. It's a traffic-free beeline toward one of the

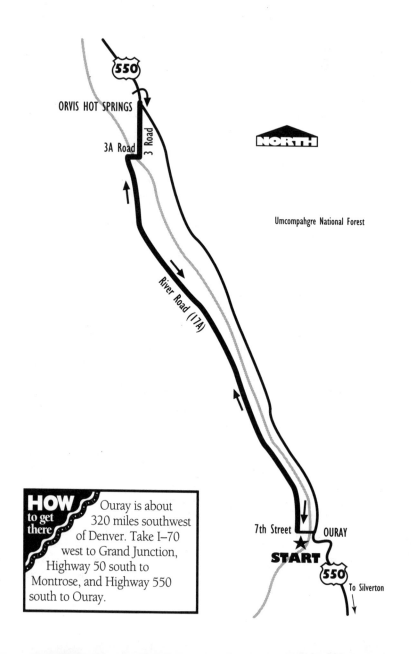

550

ORVIS HOT SPRINGS

3A Road

3 Road

NORTH

Umcompahgre National Forest

River Road (17A)

7th Street

OURAY

★ **START**

550

To Silverton

HOW to get there
Ouray is about 320 miles southwest of Denver. Take I–70 west to Grand Junction, Highway 50 south to Montrose, and Highway 550 south to Ouray.

0.0	Start at Ouray town center, Seventh and Main. Head west on Seventh toward the river.
0.2	Turn right onto River Road (Route 17).
10.0	Turn right onto 3A Road.
10.0	Take an immediate left onto 3 Road.
11.0	Arrive at Orvis. Turn around and retrace steps.
22.0	Return to Ouray.

neatest developed hot springs in the state. Start at the gas station at Seventh and Main in Ouray. Head west for 3 blocks on Seventh and take a right at the T. Head north to ride through a camping area with the river, emerald green from mineral content, on your right.

You'll slowly gravitate through a lush sandstone valley, with hillsides carpeted in gambel oak. You might see a marmot or an eagle, but not many people. Pass by a goat ranch and climb over a knoll with some fancy new houses. Then descend into flat ranching and farming country, crossing the occasional cattle guard, red-wing blackbirds perched on fence posts. At the San Juan Guest Ranch (marked by a huge stone and log gateway), take a right on the 3A Road and a quick left onto County 3 Road.

Just past some old greenhouses and a giant propane tank is the Orvis Hot Springs (admission $7.00 in 1994; call 970–626–5324). From the front it looks like an unassuming cabin, but get inside and you could stay all day (or at least all afternoon, as we did). Indoors there are hot tubs, massage rooms, and a medium-temperature soaking pool nicely sculpted from local stone. The owners view this as a circle-of-friends operation—be sure to respect their rules.

Outside, a stone path leads through colorful flowerbeds to a sunken pool separated from a pasture by a split-rail fence. Sit on a rock ledge and gaze at the distant San Juans and at hummingbirds dancing among the flowers. You can also camp out back or rent a room here.

The ride back follows the same route you took down the valley. It's slightly more uphill (some 700 feet in elevation gain), but the views of the 14ers embracing Ouray are transfixing. If you need to soak sore muscles again, try the million-gallon Ouray Hot Springs Pool at ride's end. For information on other rides in the area, inquire at Ouray Mountain Sports, 722 Main Street, Ouray 81427, or call (970) 325–4284.

Ridgway Ranch Loop

Distance:	12.9 miles
Approximate pedaling time:	90 minutes
Terrain:	Rolling between about 6,900 and 7,400 feet
Surface:	Paved and dirt 2-lane roads
Things to see:	Ranch country, views of San Juans
Facilities:	All in Ridgway

Until recently, except for some eccentric railroad history, the most notable thing that you could say about Ridgway was, "It's not spelled with an *e*." The ranching and railroad town, founded in 1891, was known in the 1940s for good hunting and fishing as well as "a scattering of frame cottages . . . overshadowed by the smoke-blackened, red brick shops of the Rio Grande Southern Railroad," according to *Colorado: A Guide to the Highest State* (1941).

The belching smoke disappeared after the railroad—with Ridgway as the hub—was dismantled in 1952. The town should have dried up and blown away like tumbleweed. Instead, today's Ridgway finds itself a healthful development hotspot, even glamorous in a way, as celebrities like Ralph Lauren and Dennis Weaver acquire ranches cradled by the San Juans. There's also a glistening new state park built around a 5-mile-long, Mediterranean-blue reservoir, completed only in 1987.

So we went expecting mini-malls and Spagos downtown. Guess what? Ridgway's still quiet and unspoiled. The population totals all of 820 souls. The main signs of growth are tract mansions sprouting in former pasture and grassland. Otherwise, here's a short, easy ride through purple-sage prairie and ranches of the Old West.

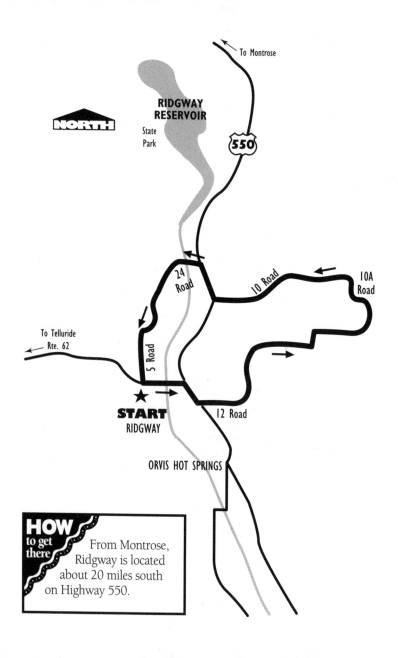

DIRECTIONS at a glance

0.0 Start at Ridgway Town Park, Sherman Street.
0.5 Turn right onto Highway 550.
0.7 Turn left onto 12 Road.
2.7 Bear right at fork to stay on 12 Road.
3.7 Bear left to stay on 12 Road.
5.2 Turn left onto 10A Road.
7.2 Turn left onto 10 Road.
9.7 Turn right onto Highway 550.
10.5 Turn left onto 24 Road.
11.7 Turn left onto 5 Road (Stringtown Road).
12.7 Turn left onto Main Street.
12.9 Return to Ridgway Town Park.

Start at the west end of downtown and head east on Main Street. (Not that you'll get confused, but east–west streets have men's names, and north–south are named for women.) At an intersection, turn right onto Route 62 (a left takes you toward Telluride) and immediately left on the 12 Road. You'll find a broad, shale-based valley dotted with haybales, with views of the San Juans to the south and east. The bumpy dirt/gravel road takes you right into the shadow of craggy, volcanic peaks.

Turn left at an UNCOMPAHGRE NATIONAL FOREST ACCESS sign near a dry wash. Start to climb past a field of stacked white boxes. These are bee houses. The road climbs to offer views of mesas dotted with piñon pine. At the next intersection, turn left on Route 10 for a sweeping view of the Cimarron Mountains and Uncompahgre Valley. Coast downhill to Highway 550 and turn right. Take this state road north briefly, and turn left onto Route 24. Just after you turn, a short greenway off to the right leads to a fishing area.

Keep your eyes peeled for the unmarked Stringtown Road (or 5 Road), identifiable by a bridge over Dallas Creek. Now you're heading south. Mount Sneffels and the San Juans are visible in the distance beyond Ouray. Climb along the creek, lined by tall willows, into open range. Smell the fresh-cut hay. (But this panorama is starting to be filled in by bombastic new houses.) Near town, Stringtown Road becomes Amelia Street. Coast by a white picket fence on the way into town.

An option may await by the summer of 1995. Construction may be complete on an off-road bike lane/nature trail through 3,260-acre Ridgway State Park, just 10 minutes north of town on Highway 550. Call the park at (970) 626–5822 for details.

Crested Butte Circuit

Distance:	14 or 23 miles
Approximate pedaling time:	2–3 hours
Terrain:	River valleys
Surface:	Paved highway, gravel, some single-track switchbacks
Things to see:	Historic mining town, working ranches, mountain vistas
Facilities:	All in town

Many Coloradans contend that Crested Butte is the last ski town not wrecked by pretense, rising land prices, and eight-story condos tarted up with quasi-Tyrolean gingerbread. Even the governor has spoken of the need to save this gem of a region. Indeed, the town's isolation—ensured by its dead-end location in an 8,900-foot valley—already offers a degree of protection from resort-itis. You'll see plenty of tourists, but sense of community remains strong.

Most of Crested Butte's distinctive architecture survives, too: brightly colored creations built by Croatian and Slovene miners in a jaunty, cartoonish version of Victorian. A National Historic District, the former coal- and silver-mining village has been restored down to the last clapboard. Garishly painted houses and shops rival San Francisco's painted ladies.

There's plenty to do besides look: Crested Butte hosts a microbrewery, wildflower festival, Harley weekend, summer theater, and arts center.

Most of all, though, Crested Butte and the adjacent resort community of Mount Crested Butte have become famous for mountain biking. The early miners cut burro trails far into adjacent 12,000-foot

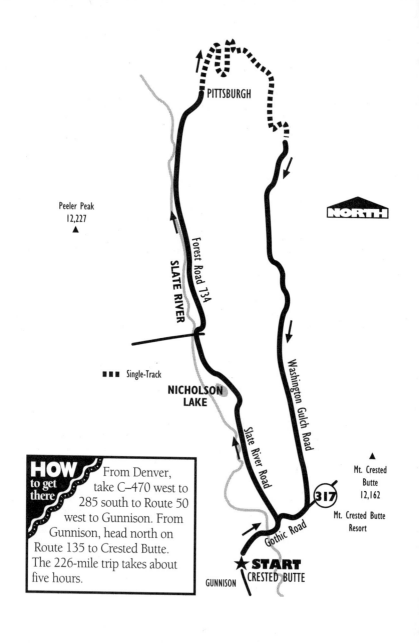

PITTSBURGH

Peeler Peak
12,227
▲

Forest Road 134

SLATE RIVER

Washington Gulch Road

NORTH

■■■ Single-Track

**NICHOLSON
LAKE**

Slate River Road

Mt. Crested
Butte
12,162
▲

317

Mt. Crested Butte
Resort

HOW
to get
there
From Denver,
take C–470 west to
285 south to Route 50
west to Gunnison. From
Gunnison, head north on
Route 135 to Crested Butte.
The 226-mile trip takes about
five hours.

Gothic Road

★ **START**
CRESTED BUTTE

GUNNISON

DIREC-TIONS at a glance

0.0 Start at the town information center at the corner of Elk Avenue and Route 135. Head east on the paved road toward Mount Crested Butte ski resort.

0.8 Turn left onto Slate River Road at FOREST ACCESS sign.

7.0 Either turn round and retrace steps or continue onto Washington Gulch route.

10.0 Pass through the old mining town of Pittsburgh.

11.0 Just past Pittsburgh, bear right onto a single-track trail heading north.

13.0 Bear right at a Forest Service sign for Washington Gulch Road.

21.0 Turn right onto pavement at Gothic Road.

23.0 Return to town center.

mountains. Today these paths contribute to hundreds of miles of trails through aspen forests and extravagant wildflower meadows. The sport is celebrated annually each July during Fat Tire Week, which includes a slalom race and mountain-bike rodeo. Crested Butte is also home to the Mountain Bike Hall of Fame, at 126 Elk Avenue. There the mid-1970s photos of hirsute men in flannel shirts astride fat-tire prototypes look as distant as tintypes.

Start the ride on Elk Avenue. Take time to explore the whimsical buildings along the main drag. There's the Town Hall, designed in 1883 by an Eastern European immigrant; the perfect Carpenter Gothic of St. Patrick Church; a two-story outhouse; and Tony's Conoco, a kind of living museum that's home to the world's largest elk rack (among elk that have been shot down, anyway).

Turn left at the town information center (two of the area's eight bike shops with rentals are on your left) onto the main road toward Mount Crested Butte. In less than a mile, turn left on the Slate River Road at a FOREST ACCESS sign. The Slate River route, local bikes assured me, is the easiest and most scenic introduction to Crested

Butte's pleasures. Except for a few dirt bikes kicking up dust, I certainly enjoyed my ride.

A thunderstorm stewing on the peaks of the Ruby Range made for a biting headwind. The valley is "multi-use" ranch country within Gunnison National Forest. In other words, cows share space with bottomlands as the river coils through wet meadows, beaver ponds, and aspen stands. At midride I met a bespectacled cowboy (he resembled Teddy Roosevelt) in a duster. Astride a cinnamon-colored horse, he was rounding up hundreds of cows aided by whistle-trained border collies. I told him I had seen the dogs herd only sheep in England and Ireland. He squinted in disbelief and said, "They're *bred* to herd cows."

If a 14-mile round-trip is your limit, turn back at the sign for Gunsight Pass and retrace steps to Crested Butte. Otherwise, follow the directions for some vigorous single-track to Washington Gulch (site of a $350,000 gold strike in the 1880s) to complete a 23-mile loop. The ride crests out at about 10,200 feet. Not a family ride, unless you're the LeMonds.

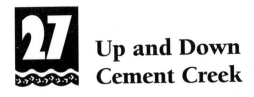

Up and Down Cement Creek

Distance:	10.4+ miles
Approximate pedaling time:	1 hour
Terrain:	Steady rise from subalpine forest to mountain meadows, with swift descent
Surface:	Gravel/dirt Jeep road
Things to see:	The best backcountry
Facilities:	Water and pit toilets at Cement Creek Campground

Seven miles southeast from Crested Butte, the Cement Creek Valley offers some of the best dirt-road riding I found in a summer of looking. At midday you might share territory with dust-kicking Jeeps and motorbikes, but all was quiet in the early morning when I rode.

Start at a U.S. Forest Service campground, 4 miles off Route 135 on Forest Road 740. A few paces from the creek, our campsite was shaded by spruces and framed by a pair of jagged sandstone mountains. Turn right out of the campground and start climbing on a windy dirt/gravel road. For a time the roadsides are fairly open and dotted with clumps of sage, fireweed, penstemon, orange paintbrush, and cow parsnip, set against aspens and red-rock cliffs.

The creek narrows. Suddenly you're in a dark canyon, with water tumbling down stone steps. This canyon spills out from a mountain bog where the creek is subsumed by thickets of willows and red-twig dogwood. Swallows flit about the rustic shed buildings of Cement Creek Ranch. After a mile traversing flat wetlands, the road climbs again, through 90-foot-tall aspens, until the creek narrows into an even deeper gorge.

A series of switchbacks past campsites leads to a bridge over Ce-

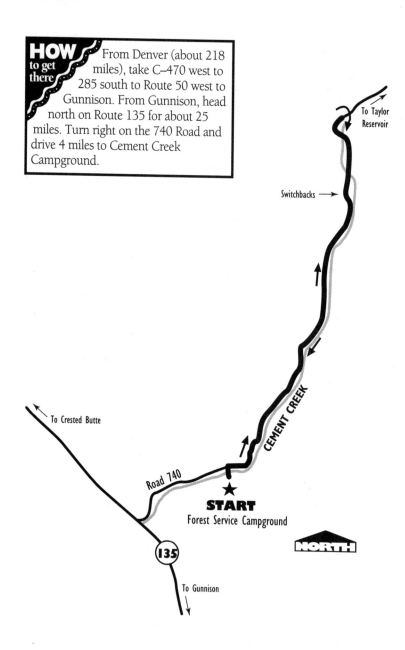

HOW to get there

From Denver (about 218 miles), take C–470 west to 285 south to Route 50 west to Gunnison. From Gunnison, head north on Route 135 for about 25 miles. Turn right on the 740 Road and drive 4 miles to Cement Creek Campground.

To Taylor Reservoir

Switchbacks →

To Crested Butte

CEMENT CREEK

Road 740

★
START
Forest Service Campground

NORTH

135

To Gunnison

DIREC-TIONS at a glance

0.0 Start at Cement Creek Campground.

2.2 Pass Cement Creek Ranch.

5.0 Cross bridge over Cement Creek.

5.2 Midpoint of ride (and end of climb) in wet meadow rimmed by peaks. Take in the view and turn around.

Option

Starting in Crested Butte, head south on Route 135 and turn left onto Road 740.

---

ment Creek. You climb past a waterfall on your left onto yet another shelf comprising a huge wet meadow, rimmed by peaks. Here I turned back (my turn to make breakfast). Other bikers and my topo map told me that the road continues for quite a while until it becomes single-track high in the Elk Mountains and then descends into the Taylor River Valley. My map also showed natural hot springs along the creek, although I couldn't find them. You might ask about them at the Taylor River/Cebolla District Forest Service Office, 216 North Colorado St., Gunnison, CO 81230, or call (970) 641–0471.

I did the ride before 7:00 A.M. on a July morning. The entire trip was above 9,000 feet, topping off at about 10,500. It was cold enough to make me wish for winter gloves.

To add 14 miles to the round-trip, start in Crested Butte, head south on 135, and turn left onto 740 Road.

Steamboat:
Biking in Ski Town

Distance:	10 miles round-trip
Approximate pedaling time:	2 hours
Terrain:	Flat river valley
Surface:	Paved bike path and dirt road
Things to see:	Historic town with hot springs, quiet section of Yampa River, wetlands, mountain views
Facilities:	Hotels, restaurants, restrooms

Before Aspen glittered or planned-to-the-ashtrays Vail unfurled as neatly as freshly set linens, Steamboat was *the* ski area in Colorado. The town of 6,000 year-round residents at about 6,600 feet in elevation sits in a valley ringed by 12,000-foot mountains. The valley receives 325 inches of snow—25 feet—annually. Local skier Carl Howelsen instantly popularized the sport by making a 110-foot jump before a stunned crowd in 1913. Since then Steamboat has produced dozens of Olympic Team skiers. The name "Ski Town USA" is actually trademarked.

But there's more to Steamboat than lift lines and champagne powder. The summer climate is ideal for exploring the flat Yampa Valley by bike. Most of it is quiet ranch country. You can dip in the river. One of the last unfettered waterways, the Yampa was named for the Yamparika Ute tribe, who hied it for Utah under duress after 1880.

Skies tend toward the opalescent; the smells of sun-baked pine and sage fill the air. More than 150 medicinal hot springs await fatigued cyclists. They range in temperature from 58 to 152 degrees. A few are public; most have been developed as private spas. (See chapter 29 for a ride featuring a visit to Strawberry Park Hot Springs, near the Mount Zirkel Wilderness.)

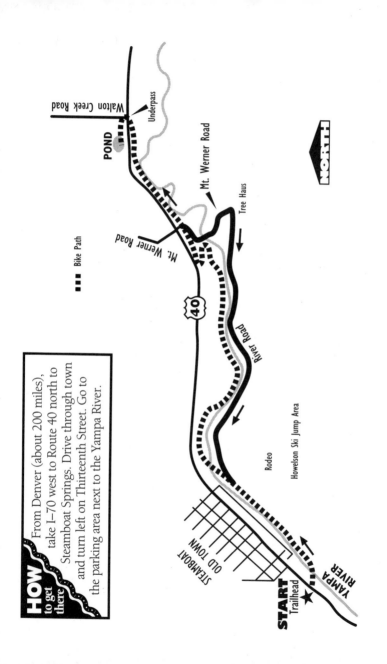

HOW to get there

From Denver (about 200 miles), take I-70 west to Route 40 north to Steamboat Springs. Drive through town and turn left on Thirteenth Street. Go to the parking area next to the Yampa River.

Bike Path

NORTH

Walton Creek Road

Underpass

POND

Mt. Werner Road

Tree Haus

Mt. Werner Road

40

River Road

Rodeo

Howelson Ski Jump Area

STEAMBOAT OLD TOWN

YAMPA RIVER

START Trailhead

DIRECTIONS at a glance

0.0 Trailhead of Yampa River Trail. Head south. Cross Yampa River on bridge.

5.0 Trail ends near Walton Creek Park. Turn around.

6.0 Turn left onto Mount Werner Road.

6.5 Turn right onto River Road.

8.5 Turn right onto Fifth Street and take an immediate left onto bike path.

10.0 Return to start.

The name Steamboat is misleading. Legend goes that a trio of French trappers stumbled into the valley and heard a chugging noise that reminded them of a Mississippi paddle wheeler. The sound emanated from a rock cave above a spring, until 1908, when railroad baron David Moffat had the chamber dynamited to build a grade for the Denver, Northwestern & Pacific Railroad.

Steamboat has worked hard to diversify its tourism base. Everything from shopping to snowmobile tours compete with slope time. There are weekend rodeos in summer and a vintage sports-car race over Labor Day attracts hundreds of MGs, DeLoreans, and Gullwings to town. Shops renting mountain bikes provide passage to the million-acre Routt National Forest.

This family ride starts at the town's northwest end, near a steamboat-theme playground at the trailhead for the Yampa River Core Trail. Built after 1991 with $2 million in bond moneys, this nicely engineered cement path runs for 5 miles. Plans are afoot to extend this system throughout the valley. Before de-biking, dip a digit into the fragrant sulphur springs by the side of the trail (the rotten-eggs smell quickly becomes familiar here). The city does not prohibit bathing here, but they don't recommend it, for sanitary reasons.

Pass by West Lincoln Park, with its landmark elk statue, and then through a picnic area on the site where the area's original homesteader, a Missourian named James H. Crawford, built a cabin. The river is on your right. Across the water the old train depot has been converted to the town's art center.

The trail parallels the backside of Steamboat's Old Town, about 12 blocks of Lincoln Avenue. The river swirls through rapids and eddies populated by kayaks and inner tubes in summer. After crossing a bridge, run parallel to the rodeo grounds and Howelsen Hill, where the Norwegian Carl made his amazing jump on a homemade halfpipe in 1913. The spot doesn't look that different today. Most ski development has occurred on the sunnier, western-facing slopes. In the distance, ridges are cloaked by lodgepole pine and aspen with peak "fall" foliage in early- to mid-September.

Upon leaving this busy town, the views open up. The river meanders and widens into marshes. You're likely to see red-winged blackbirds clinging to bulrushes. Some thoughtful Johnny Wildflowerseed has planted patches of Mexican hats and sunflowers along the path's edge. Rollerbladers are out in force. In winter bald eagles are known to roost in trees overlooking the Yampa. You can get a look on your bike because the city plows the path.

Pass Yampa River Park, designed for picnics and kayak/canoe putins (about 2 miles of the Yampa is navigable by open boats). To the left you're looking at the sprawling ski areas of Steamboat Village, a 2,500-acre development begun in 1963 that takes advantage of Sunshine, Storm, Thunderhead, and Christie peaks, areas with huge vertical drops.

About 3 miles from town, you come upon a controversial new landmark: "The Gates of Asopus," a sculpture by Seattle artist John Young. Some twenty massive slabs of Colorado granite suspended by cables flank both sides of the trail. The National Endowment for the Arts–funded piece is loved, hated, or just misunderstood in town, says Nancy Kramer of the Arts Council.

Just beyond a highway underpass near the fishing hole at Walton Creek Park, the trail ends. Turn around and retrace your steps to Mount Werner Road. Take a left and cross the Yampa. At about ½ mile, at a T intersection near a subdivision called Tree Haus, turn right onto River Road. This untrafficked, winding dirt lane takes you back to town on low bluffs overlooking the rocky Yampa. At Fifth Street, turn right and immediately left to rejoin the bike path and return to the starting point.

I did the ride on a 70-degree Labor Day, with my daughter in tow in a bike trailer. We escaped the roar of racing sports cars downtown and found several playgrounds en route. It's as easy a ride as any. An employee at the Sore Saddle bike shop, near the path at Twelfth and Yampa, recommended studded mountain-bike tires if you ride the trail in winter.

A Haul Up to Strawberry Hot Springs

Distance:	14 miles round-trip
Approximate pedaling time:	3 hours
Terrain:	Gradual descent gives way to major climb
Surface:	Paved city streets, 2-lane country road, narrow dirt road with switchbacks
Things to see:	Historic neighborhoods of Steamboat Springs, quiet ranching valley, aspen forest, great views of Yampa Valley, natural hot springs
Facilities:	None between town and hot springs

In a state packed with beautiful hot springs, Strawberry Hot Springs Park is among the choicest. A series of rock pools, waterfalls, and cliffs enveloped by wildflowers and aspens, and a short hike from the Mount Zirkel wilderness, the springs take advantage of a natural flow of 150-degree mineral waters mixed in with mountain stream water to create a perfect 104-degree balm.

But you have to sweat to get there.

The ride starts in downtown Steamboat, where Twelfth Street meets the river trail at Yampa Road. Check out the Sore Saddle bike shop across the street. This free-form structure (it resembles a stack of mashed potatoes) is a former wood-chip incinerator that the bike shop owners bought for a dollar and moved to this site. Stop in. They've got free maps and many ideas about area routes.

Head southeast on the trail and turn left onto Seventh Street. After crossing busy Lincoln Avenue, enjoy a look at Steamboat's older bungalows, many fashioned from smooth river stones and planted with

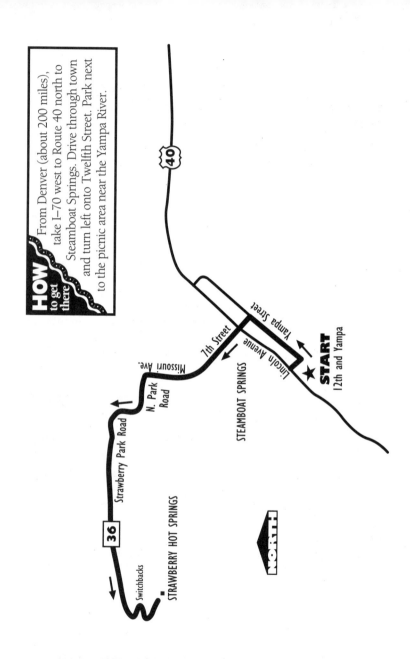

HOW to get there

From Denver (about 200 miles), take I-70 west to Route 40 north to Steamboat Springs. Drive through town and turn left onto Twelfth Street. Park next to the picnic area near the Yampa River.

40

Yampa Street

7th Street

Lincoln Avenue

Missouri Ave.

N. Park Road

Strawberry Park Road

STEAMBOAT SPRINGS

START
12th and Yampa

36

Switchbacks

STRAWBERRY HOT SPRINGS

NORTH

0.0 Start at Twelfth and Yampa in Steamboat (across from Sore Saddle bike shop). Head north on Yampa.

0.3 Turn left onto Seventh Street.

0.9 Turn right onto Missouri.

1.1 Turn left onto North Park (becomes County Road 36).

4.1 Cross bridge (road turns to dirt).

6.1 High point of ride (7,500 feet).

7.1 Arrive at Strawberry Park Hot Springs. Reverse these directions to return to town.

14.2 Return to start in Steamboat.

Colorado wildflowers and groves of aspen. In 4 blocks turn right onto Missouri. Three more blocks and it's left onto North Park.

That's it for the town. You're out in ranch country on County Road 36. The renowned Perry-Mansfield Dance Camp is on your left. The road climbs gently for a time, past fenceposts, pastures, and log homes. Magpies hover like totem figures.

Then come to a bridge over a creek. The road surface changes from paved asphalt to dirt and a 2-mile climb commences. Aspens and pines provide shade. You'll probably see woodpeckers darting among the trees. After a mile of steady ascent, begin a series of earnest switchbacks. (Many cyclists walk this section.) The summit reveals a broad vista of the Yampa Valley. From here it's a mile downhill, on a sandy dirt road, to Strawberry Hot Springs. Admission in the summer of 1995 was $5.00 for adults and $2.00 for children. Facilities are simple (you change in a tipi), and they may not have drinking water available, so carry your own.

The ride down is wild, steep, swift. You should be cocksure of your mountain-riding abilities before undertaking it (you can probably hitch a ride down with a fellow bather). It's also a blast. You'll be back in town in twenty minutes.

I did this ride on a hot Labor Day weekend with kid and trailer in tow. Aspens were beginning to mellow. Giant ferns along the road were going to rust. Despite the nice scenery, however, it's not a trek I'd recommend as a family outing; the ascent is too difficult for children. Walking the switchbacks was hard with my load. My feet were sliding out from beneath me on what felt like a 20 percent grade, with a loose, pebbly surface. Riding down hauling fifty pounds would have been suicidal. Instead, I left the crew at the springs and cruised down to Steamboat alone to pick up the car.

Leadville-Turquoise Loop

Distance:	27 miles
Approximate pedaling time:	3 hours
Terrain:	Fairly flat, but high elevation (all 10,000+ feet)
Surface:	Paved roads
Things to see:	Historic mining town, Mount Massive, Mount Elbert, Turquoise Lake
Facilities:	Hotels, restaurants, restrooms in Leadville; eight campgrounds with water, bathrooms around Turquoise Lake

Honestly named, Janus-faced Leadville, the highest incorporated city in the United States at 10,152 feet, remains a regal boom–bust town. Once Colorado's second-largest city, Leadville was built in grandiose fashion on the backs of extravagant gold and silver camps and from vast extracts of lead, zinc, and manganese. Yet "when work is slack," noted the 1941 account, *Colorado: A Guide to the Highest State,* "Leadville has almost the appearance . . . of a quiet country town that has known no greater excitement than a dog fight."

Things are pretty quiet these days as the town awaits a gathering tourism boom. One attraction is its huge, gaudy Victorian historic district. Another is the legacy of ore diva Baby Jane Tabor, who tended the Matchless Mine until well past its (and her own) prime. She froze to death in a tiny cabin next to the mine in 1935.

Some of Leadville's sights are as mesmerizing as a train wreck. You can't pull your eyes away. Sickly yellow tailings piles, collapsing shafts, and rusted headframes poking up on corners in town are mere

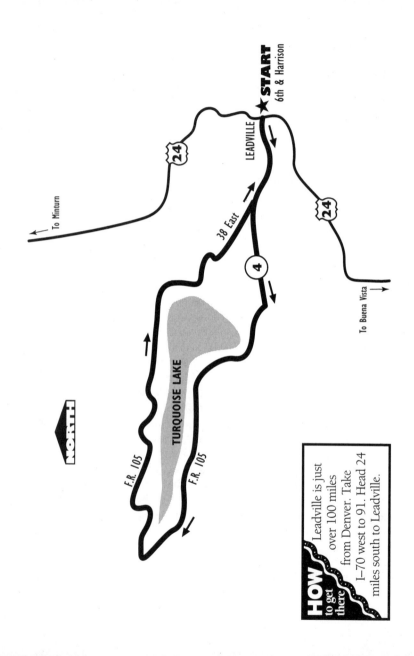

DIREC-TIONS at a glance

0.0 Start at Sixth and Harrison in downtown Leadville. Head west on Sixth through the town's only traffic light.

0.5 At a T intersection, turn right onto State Road 4.

2.0 Bear left at a fork. Begin loop around Turquoise Lake.

23.0 At a fork, bear left onto 38 east.

26.5 At T, turn right onto North Harrison Avenue.

27.0 Return to start.

prologue to the area's human-caused landscape devastation, where mining has filed down entire mountains.

Many of Leadville's historic mines are concentrated east of town, where I was unable to develop a suitable circuit. This ride (based on a popular citizens' race held in August) takes advantage of Leadville's other face: a peerless natural setting, best seen by heading west around Turquoise Lake. You can enjoy views of a wilderness area and the state's highest peaks in the Sawatch Range. Beware the weather: Locals wouldn't blink at a July Fourth blizzard.

Start downtown at Leadville's only traffic light, at Sixth and Harrison. Some red-brick buildings, like the Delaware Hotel on Harrison, have been flawlessly restored; others are simply tarted up and beset with ventures like the "Baby Dough" Bakery. Head west on Sixth. In ½ mile turn right at a T intersection near a recreation center. State Road 4 heads directly to the lake.

Turquoise is prettier than most reservoirs, owing to its scalloped shape and alpine setting. Either a "sportsman's paradise" or an industrial "storage unit," depending on your point of view, it's part of the colossal Frying Pan–Arkansas Project. This network of dams and pipes muscles water for irrigation and power down both sides of the Continental Divide.

At a fork, bear left to start a counterclockwise loop around the

lake. Mount Massive (elevation 14,421 feet) is due southwest, state champion Elbert (14,433 feet) due south. A smooth, two-lane road skims the lakeshore through a Bureau of Land Management mining area and then into San Isabel National Forest. After completing the loop return to town on Route 38 east.

Cycling Organizations

Adventure Cycling Association (formerly Bikecentennial), P.O. Box 8308-PR, Missoula, MT 59807; phone (406) 721–1776.

Banana Belt Fat Tracks Mountain Biking Club, c/o Otero Cyclery, Salida, CO; phone (719) 539–6704.

Bicycle Colorado, 5249 East Eastman Avenue, Denver, CO 80222-7550; phone (303) 756–2535.

Bolder Bicycle Commuters, P.O. Box 1277, Boulder, CO 80306; phone (303) 499–7466.

Boulder Off-Road Alliance, phone (303) 441–5262.

Breckenridge Fat-Tire Society, P.O. Box 2845, Breckenridge, CO 80424; phone (970) 453–5548.

Colorado Bicycle Coalition, 191 University Boulevard, Box 261, Denver, CO 80202; (303) 355–5451.

Colorado Bicycle Industry Coalition, P.O. Box 19673, Boulder CO 80308; (303) 545–6679.

Colorado Springs Bicycle Club, P.O. Box 49602, Colorado Springs, CO 80949; phone (719) 594–6354.

Denver Bicycle Touring Club, P.O. Box 8973, Denver, CO; phone (303) 756-7240.

Durango Wheel Club, 949 Main Avenue, Durango, CO 81301; phone (970) 247–4066.

International Mountain Biking Association (IMBA), 1634 Walnut Street, Suite 301, Boulder, CO 80302; phone (303) 545–9011.

National Off-Road Bicycle Association (NORBA), 1 Olympic Plaza, Colorado Springs, CO 80909; phone (719) 578–4717.

Rock & Mud, P.O. Box 3220, Avon, CO 81620; phone (970) 827–4203.

Team Evergreen Bicycle Club, P.O. Box 3804, Evergreen, CO 80439-3804; (970) 674–6048.

Winter Park Fat Tire Society, P.O. Box 1337, Winter Park, CO 80482; phone (970) 726–4118.

Bicycling Maps

Colorado Trails Books and Maps Catalogue, P.O. Box 5157, Wheatridge, CO 80033; phone (303) 232–8243. Dozens of books and maps available by mail.

Boulder Map Gallery, 1708 Thirteenth Street, Boulder, CO 80302; phone (303) 444–1406. Maps and books for all seasons.

Trails Illustrated Bike Series Maps, P.O. Box 3610, Evergreen, CO 80439-3425; phone (800) 962–1643 or (metro Denver) (303) 670–3457. Topo maps printed on plastic for durability.

The Colorado Trails Guides. Series of free maps published by the Colorado Division of Parks & Outdoor Recreation. Available at many state parks and bike shops.

Bicycling Colorado. Statewide map prepared by Colorado Department of Highways, 4201 East Arkansas Avenue, Denver, CO 80222.

Colorado Atlas & Gazetteer: Topo Maps of the Entire State. $14.95, 103 maps in one binder. DeLorme Publishing Company, P.O. Box 298-6700, Freeport, ME 04032; phone (800) 227–1656 to order by phone. Available in many stores.

Go Boulder Open Space/Parks and Trails Map. Available from Go Boulder, 2018 Eleventh Street, Boulder, CO 80306; phone (303) 441–3216.

Mountain Bike Map—Boulder County, Latitude 40. $8.50. Available at many bike shops.

Winter Park/Fraser Valley Mountain Bike Trail Guide. Published by the Winter Park Resort and the Winter Park/Fraser Valley Chamber of Commerce. Free at local bike shops.

Crested Butte/Mount Crested Butte Mountain Bike Trails, by Laura Guccione, 1993. $8.95 at local bike shops.

Steamboat Springs Bicycle Trails Map. Free at local bike shops.

The Summit County Bike Path and Mountain Bike Map. Summit County Government. $2.00. Available at local bike shops.

Glenwood Springs Hike & Mountain Bicycle Trail Map. Free from the Glenwood Springs Chamber Resort Association; phone (800) 221–0098.

Bicycling Books

Alley, Jean, and Hartley Alley. *Colorado Cycling Guide,* Pruett Publishing, 1990.

Coello, Dennis. *Bicycle Touring Colorado,* Northland Publishing, 1989.

Dowling, Mark. *Bike with a View: Colorado's Front Range and Central Mountains,* Concepts in Publishing, 1994.

Nelson, David. *Rocky Mountain News Ride Guide: Favorite Colorado Bike Routes from the Weekly Column,* Denver Publishing, 1993.

————— . *Rocky Mountain News Ride Guide II: 36 New Colorado Bicycle Routes from the Weekly Column,* Denver Publishing, 1993.

Rich, Dave. *Boulderides, The Mountain Biking Guide to Boulder, Colorado,* Little Rose Publishing, 1993.

————— . *Tellurides: The Mountain Bike Guide to Telluride, Colorado,* Wayfinder Press, 1994.

Rossetter, Laura. *Mountain Biking Colorado's Historic Mining Districts,* Fulcrum Publishing, 1991.

————— . *The Mountain Bike Guide to Summit County, Colorado,* Sage Creek Press, 1993.

Stoehr, William. *Bicycling the Backcountry: Mountain Bike Guide to Colorado,* Pruett Publishing, 1987.

Wilson, Marcus. *Biking Ouray: Mountain Biking Guide to Ridgway and Ouray, Colorado,* Wayfinder Press, 1993.

Wockner, Gary. *Gold Hill and Back: A Mountain Bike Escapade,* B-Store Press, 1992.

Other Books

Cahill, Rick. *Colorado Hot Springs Guide,* Pruett Publishers, 1994.

Chronic, Halka. *Roadside Geology of Colorado,* Mountain Press, 1990.

Colorado Writers' Project. *Colorado: A Guide to the Highest State,* Hastings House, 1941.

Freed, Elaine. *Preserving the Great Plains and Rocky Mountains,* National Trust for Historic Preservation, 1992.

Harding, Matt, and Freddie Snalam. *Get Out of Town! A Comprehensive Guide to Outdoor Activities in the Boulder Area,* All Points Publishing, 1994.

Jacobs, Randy. *The Colorado Trail: Official Guide Book,* Westcliffe Publishers, 1992.

————— ed., *Guide to the Colorado Mountains,* Colorado Mountain Club, 1992.

Kleinsorge, Martin G. *Exploring Colorado's State Parks,* University Press of Colorado, 1992.

Noel, Thomas J., Paul F. Mahoney, and Richard E. Stevens. *Historical Atlas of Colorado,* University of Oklahoma Press, 1994.

Bicycle Rentals

Boulder area

University Bicycles, Ninth and Pearl, Boulder; phone (303) 444–4196.

Doc's Ski and Sport, 629E South Broadway, Boulder; phone (303) 499–0963.

High Wheeler, 1015 Pearl Street, Boulder (tandems only); phone (303) 442–5588.

Louisville Cyclery, 1032 South Boulder Road, Louisville; phone (303) 665–6343.

Breckenridge

Kodi Rafting and Bikes, Bell Tower Shops; phone (970) 453–2194.

Racer's Edge, Main Street; phone (970) 453–0995.

Buena Vista Area

The Trailhead, 707 Highway 24 North, Buena Vista; phone (719) 395–8001.

Otero Cyclery, 108 F Street, Salida; phone (719) 539–6704.

Outdoor Headwaters, North F Street, Salida; phone (719) 539–4506.

Pedal Pusher, 513 East Highway 50, Salida; phone (719) 539–7498.

Crested Butte

The Alpiner, 419 Sixth Street; phone (970) 349–5210.

Alpine Outside, 635 Sixth Street; phone (970) 349–5011.

Paradise Bikes, 232 Elk Avenue; phone (970) 349–6324.

Mount Crested Butte

Crested Butte Sports, Evergreen Building; phone (970) 349–7516.

Gene Taylors Sports, 19 Emmons Building; phone (970) 349–5386.

Butte & Co., Treasury Building; phone (970) 349–7581.

Christy Sports, Treasury Building; phone (970) 349–6601.

Flatiron Sports, Treasury Building; phone (970) 349–6656.

Denver

Bike Broker, Inc., 1440 Market; phone (303) 893–8675.

Cycle Analyst, 722 South Pearl; phone (303) 722–3004.

Sports Rent, 560 South Holly; phone (303) 320–0222.

Durango

Hassle Free Sports, 2615 Main Avenue; phone (970) 259–3874.

Mountain Bike Specialists/The Outdoorsman, 949 Main Avenue; (970) 247–4066.

Evergreen

Paragon Sports, 2962 Highway 74; phone (970) 670–0092.

Fort Collins

Rock 'n Road Cyclery, 4206 South College; phone (970) 223–7623.
The Whistle Stop, 410 Jefferson Street; phone (970) 224–5499.
Together Tandems, 410 Jefferson Street; phone (970) 224–0330.

Frisco

Antlers Ski & Sport, 908 North Summit Boulevard; phone (970) 668–3152.

Christy Sports, 849 North Summit Boulevard; phone (970) 668–5417.

Classic Sports, Fifth and Main; phone (970) 668–0344.

Frisco City Sports, 299 Main Street; phone (970) 668–1600.

Pioneer Sports, 840 North Summit Boulevard; (970) 668–3668.

Rebel Sports, 402 Main Street; phone (970) 668–1689.

Team Managers, 121 North Summit Boulevard; phone (970) 668–3748.

Glenwood Springs

Adventure Rentals, Inc., 124 West Sixth Street at Ramada Inn; phone (970) 928–0900.

BSR Sports, 210 Seventh Street; phone (970) 945–7317.

Canyon Bikes, 319 Sixth Street (Hotel Colorado); phone (970) 945–8904.

Rock Gardens, 1308 County Road 129; phone (970) 945–6737.

Ski Sunlight Ski & Bike Shop; phone (970) 945–9425.

Ouray

Ouray Mountain Sports, 722 Main Street; (970) 325–4284.

Snow Mountain Ranch

Snow Mountain Ranch YMCA of the Rockies, P.O. Box 169, Winter Park, CO 80482; phone (970) 887–2152 (Denver line 443–4743).

Winter Park

Winter Park Sports Shop, Downtown at Kings Crossing; phone (970) 726–5554 (Denver line 573–9397).